VICTORY CELEBRATIONS

Alexander Solzhenitsyn

Victory Celebrations

A COMEDY IN FOUR ACTS
TRANSLATED FROM THE RUSSIAN BY
HELEN RAPP AND NANCY THOMAS

THE BODLEY HEAD

LONDON SYDNEY

TORONTO

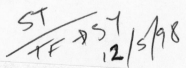
Originally published by YMCA Press, Paris, 1981
as *Pir pobediteley*

British Library Cataloguing
in Publication Data
Solzhenitsyn, Aleksandr
Victory celebrations.
I. Title   II. Pir pobediteley. *English*
891.72′44   PG3488.04
ISBN 0–370–30486–1

World copyright © Alexander Solzhenitsyn 1981
Translation © The Bodley Head Ltd
and Farrar, Straus & Giroux Inc 1983
Printed in Great Britain for
The Bodley Head Ltd
9 Bow Street, London WC2E 7AL
by Redwood Burn Ltd, Trowbridge
Set in Linotron 202 Ehrhardt.
by Wyvern Typesetting Ltd, Bristol
First published in Great Britain 1983

DRAMATIS PERSONAE

Lieutenant-Colonel BERBENCHUK, Divisional Commander, Special Army Artillery Reconnaissance

Major VANIN, Divisional Deputy Commander, Political Branch

Captain DOBROKHOTOV-MAIKOV, Staff Captain

Captain NERZHIN, Commander, Radio-Intelligence Unit

Captain LIKHARYOV, Commander, Topographical Intelligence Unit

Lieutenant GRIDNEV, accredited officer of Counter-Intelligence, SMERSH

Captain ANECHKA, Divisional Medical Officer, Vanin's wartime 'wife'

GLAFIRA, Berbenchuk's wife

GALINA

Lieutenant PROKOPOVICH, technician

Divisional PARTY ORGANISER, 'liberated'

Divisional HEAD OF CHEMICAL UNIT

Lieutenant YACHMENNIKOV, Platoon Commander in Nerzhin's unit

KATYA } , girls from the neighbouring unit
OLYA

SALIY } indistinguishable pair of Tartar Red Army
ZAMALIY ' soldiers

The divisional COOK

DYAGILEV, soldier

Radio Operator

Staff Sergeants and soldiers

The action takes place on 25th January, 1945, in East Prussia.

[5]

PUBLISHER'S NOTE

This play, in the original Russian, is in iambic verse.
The translators' notes are printed on pages 85–6.

The set for the four acts remains the same throughout. It is the hall of an ancient castle. On the right, there are several curtained windows. In front of them, there is a grand piano, a small round table and some armchairs. At the back, tall double doors, flanked by ordinary ones. All around the hall is a portrait gallery of military ancestors, and above that a musicians' gallery. To the left, there is a small table with a radio transmitter, and odd bits of furniture. Downstage a radiogram, and downstage of that a staircase leading up. From above there hangs a grand but unlit chandelier. When the current is on, a few bright bulbs fixed up temporarily in the chandelier emit a strong light.

ACT ONE

The stage is in complete darkness, apart from the red glow of the transmitter light. From the back one can hear the ringing tones of

MAIKOV: Hold on, hold on, don't drop it, chaps. You, up there with the rope.

A VOICE (*from above at the back*): The rope is holding, sir.

MAIKOV: Careful now. Saliy, some lights in here, whatever you can find. (*Quietly*) No questions asked? All's well? We'll edge it down. You, Zamaliy, where are you?

VOICE: Here, sir.

MAIKOV: Get the technician. At the double!

A variety of flickering lights appear simultaneously through the doors at the back, on the gallery, on the stairs. They are torches, lighted candelabra, candles, oil lamps and flares. They are all in motion. What gradually emerges from the darkness is an enormous wall mirror, several metres high, which reflects the lights on to the

*audience as it is slowly lowered sideways. It is being held up by
soldiers with batons and bare hands from below and by ropes from
above. In front, at the little table on the right, two female figures
are revealed.*

MAIKOV: Come on, light bearers! The torches, the candles!
All right, up there?

A VOICE (*from the gallery*): O.K. up here.

MAIKOV: Gently now. Hold it up, hold it. With your shoulder.
Catch it, catch it. Hold on!

*The mirror slips more and more on its side and finally reaches the
floor with its shiny side facing the audience. It is stood on its edge. A
pause. The ropes are being untied.*

MAIKOV: That's army discipline, that is! Right. Let's lift it.
On to the stools.

*The mirror is propped up against the stools which are there, ready
waiting.*

GALINA: What's the mirror for?

MAIKOV: Well, it's Columbus's egg. A very simple idea. But I
must confess, a bit of swank on my part. There is to be a
celebration in our unit, a big dinner, a big show, and not a
table in the hall. Got nicked, I suppose.

*A bright electric light blazes up in the chandelier, after which all
the other lights are put out and taken away, apart from two or three
forgotten candles. Some fifteen soldiers can be seen moving around
arranging things. They eventually leave. Dobrokhotov-Maikov
is a slim officer of medium height with a blond moustache and a
military bearing. He wears many medals. Now and again he
unnecessarily clanks his spurs. At the table on the right sit diminu-
tive Anechka in military uniform, and Galina, soberly dressed,
mainly in black. The radio operator is bent over the transmitter.
The mirror sparkles at the audience.*

MAIKOV (*measuring*): Not too low? (*He leans elegantly on the
carved legs of the mirror support which are now sticking forward.*)
An inspiration, dear lady (*to Galina*). You, as a pianist, will
know that it is not subject to logic. (*He gestures to the soldiers
who return from off-stage to lift the mirror on to the stools, shiny*

side upwards.) Over here, right under the chandelier. It overwhelms us, unexpectedly, menacingly! The way Surikov[1] envisaged Lady Morozova[2] as a crow on the snow, one wing aloft. Come on, Dyagilev, off with these mirror legs.

He moves away, giving orders. Dyagilev, an elderly man, strokes the mirror legs affectionately, having been told to break them off.

ANECHKA: You see, I am younger than he is by twelve years.

DYAGILEV: Got to use your head . . .

ANECHKA: Perhaps this difference is for the best?

DYAGILEV: They're pinned as well as glued . . .

RADIO OPERATOR: I'm receiving. I'm receiving.

MAIKOV (*to Dyagilev*): Stop thinking about it. Chop them off.

A sergeant enters quickly, and pointedly salutes Maikov. Prokopovich is behind him; he assumes an excessively unmilitary and gloomy pose, standing for a long time at the back, as if unnoticed by Maikov.

MAIKOV: Well, Sergeant?

SERGEANT: It's about the table cloth . . .

MAIKOV: A concert grand . . . And Gothic gloom . . . And a white table cloth . . . No, all wrong. No table cloth.

The sergeant salutes.

GALINA: My school friend and I used to devour romantic novels. But, when all's said and done, it's nothing but a sad tale of men's love withering away . . .

DYAGILEV (*continuing timidly to examine the mirror legs*): Did you say chop them off, Comrade Captain?

MAIKOV: I said off with them.

Dyagilev taps gently with the haft of his axe.

ANECHKA: So?

GALINA: So if that's inevitable, there's nothing more reassuring than an elderly husband. He'll never let you down, not ever.

MAIKOV (*moving Dyagilev aside*): Come on, Burlov, give it a bash.

Another soldier spits into his palms, and, taking the axe, knocks the mirror support off in two blows. Anechka blocks up her ears. The soldiers, under the direction of Maikov and of the sergeant, begin bringing in a vast amount of refreshments from the corridor and arranging them on plates, dishes, in decanters, in glass jars and in tins. They carry in lots of crockery, china, silver and crystal glasses, as well as flowers. The enormous "table" is covered completely with food and wine. The soldiers are trained to a T and operate with the precision of circus performers. Maikov's conducting gestures are theatrical.

MAIKOV: I'm interested to know, Prokopovich, are you an officer or a vicar's son. What have you come for?

PROKOPOVICH (*about to leave*): Excuse me, I was told you seemed to want me.

MAIKOV: "Seemed" nothing. I did want you. But you stand there like a sack of potatoes. What happened? There wasn't any light. A fault? A fuse?

PROKOPOVICH (*submissively*): a fuse . . .

MAIKOV: The men can't work in the dark. Bear that in mind. The light isn't to go out tonight for a second. Is that clear?

PROKOPOVICH (*shuffling*): My function, formally speaking . . .

MAIKOV (*in a theatrical whisper*): What did you say? Answering back? That's bad. What about your thousand a month? What about the extra ration? In Civvy Street you'd get it in the neck for that extra butter. Where do you think you are, at war, or on holiday? And who's to repair the arm of my radiogram? And who, forgive the crude image, is to keep the bloody show on the road? An Abyssinian prince, perhaps?

GALINA: But Anechka, all this fruit, this wine. Is it usual?

ANECHKA: Oh, no. We're celebrating today.

MAIKOV: I've been too soft on you as it is. Get down to work and start on the radiogram.

Thereafter Prokopovich examines the fault, comes and goes carrying a screwdriver, a soldering iron, radio components, and settles down to his repairs. Things are still being brought in to put on the mirror, but less frequently.

ANECHKA: You will, of course, join us at table. You've already met the divisional commander and his wife. As for me, you're probably thinking there's nothing in that head of hers: the way she pours her heart out the moment she enters the room.

GALINA: No, don't say that!

ANECHKA: I hardly ever get the chance. I'm always among men, a bivouac existence. I've been missing feminine company. You *will* come?

GALINA: It's a bit awkward . . .

ANECKHA: Not another word.

MAIKOV (*still making arrangements, but having heard snatches of their conversation*): And you will be the princess of the Staff ball. I'd have said you'd be the queen, but you know the size of the division . . .

ANECHKA: Go away. You have this terrible habit of interfering in women's talk.

MAIKOV: I'm going.

ANECHKA: That's almost all there'll be. No need to bother about the Head of the Chemical Unit, or the sound technician. You'll also meet the Party Organiser – not much joy there; a couple of battalion commanders, but they're nice enough chaps. There will be one other, though . . .

LIKHARYOV (*entering from the corridor, with a touch of foxtrot in his step, walks towards the radiogram. He too is wearing spurs, and has an excellent military bearing. He hums*):
Es geht alles forüber, es geht alles forbei,
Und nach jedem Dezember kommt wieder ein Mai . . .

MAIKOV: You're on the slippery slope, old son.

LIKHARYOV: Shall I choose a few records while there's time? (*Choosing*)

MAIKOV: You've forgotten your native land, your native Provence.

LIKHARYOV: I get along, while there's still a chance.

MAIKOV: Oh, Ivan, was it you
Who all these years of war
Was sweaty, torn and footsore?

LIKHARYOV (*straightening his coat*): Is my jacket all right, Comrade Captain? Not too tight in the shoulder? (*He selects some records, and carries away a batch, dancing and glancing at Galina*):

Es geht alles forüber, es geht alles forbei
Und nach jedem Dezember . . .

ANECHKA: As for me, I'm a bit shy about dressing up. Even a tiny touch of colour seems vulgar with my kind of clothes. It's sad. I'd try things on and end up wearing a military shirt. Even before the war I used to dress like a school girl. It's a pity I can't do it now.

GALINA: There're lots of things to wear, anything you like. The owner's wardrobe is . . . Come to my room.

ANECHKA: Thank you, love, I'll come. But will there be something . . .

GALINA: I'm sure there will. I used to be like you, but those Viennese taught me a thing or two.

RADIO OPERATOR: Ryazan calling. That's how it works. Kostroma calling. I'm receiving loud and clear.

MAIKOV: When are you going to change your call signal, you fool.

RADIO OPERATOR (*waving a bit of paper*): I've got them here. I just can't get used to these foreign names.

MAIKOV: "We are Scythians, we are Asiatics"[3] and yet we shovelled out the French. When the Germans barged in, we shoved them out. Hey, Prokopovich, what's your view of the Slavs?

PROKOPOVICH: I'm busy, Comrade Captain, can't you see?

MAIKOV: Oh, hell. No one to talk to.

ANECHKA: I'd like to warn you, don't call me Anechka. Address me formally. This is the army and I'm an officer . . .

GALINA: Yes, of course. Must abide by the rules.

RADIO OPERATOR: Comrade Captain, the second battery,

BZR, is leaving the battlefield and Nerzhin will be here in an hour.

(*Prokopovich has repaired the radiogram. Music.*)

MAIKOV: It took you two hours to get the order. Get your stuff out of here.

Radio operator removes his transmitter. Galina is trying to hide her excitement.

GALINA: Excuse me. I . . . I can't have heard it right. What name did he say, what name?

ANECHKA: Which? Nerzhin?

GALINA: Yes.

ANECHKA: Do you know him?

GALINA: No. That is . . . I used to know someone . . . And BZR?

ANECKHA: I would decipher it for you, but I mustn't. Our division is on a secret mission.

GALINA: Where's he from?

ANECHKA: Who?

GALINA: Nerzhin.

ANECHKA: from Rostov.

GALINA: Can't be him then.

ANECHKA: Aren't you from his district? Didn't you mention . . .

GALINA: You must have misheard . . .

ANECHKA: Really? Well, maybe. (*With sympathy*) Can I be of help? You seem worried. I've been watching you all evening – something is oppressing you, some fear, some anguish . . .

GALINA: You have a kind heart. Thank you for that. But in this no-one can help me.

The table is ready, although Maikov is still moving things around. The soldiers have stopped going backwards and forwards. Prokopovich is back working on the radiogram. The music is cut short. Glafira comes in quickly; she is rather portly; her hands are full with a gleaming kettle and something wrapped up in a cloth.

GLAFIRA: Who's here? Oh, it's you, you poor suffering thing! You've been saved, but how many are there still awaiting liberation, wretched slaves. I took you to my heart – close, so close. I'm all a-tremble.

ANECHKA: Are you ill?

GLAFIRA: How I hate them. Just let me get hold of some fucking Fritz: I'll scratch his eyes out. To seize this wonderful girl! Nazis! A slave market!

PROKOPOVICH: Up – to get radio stations: down – for records.

GLAFIRA: Staff Captain! Tell him off! Why do the lights fail all the time?

Maikov dismisses Prokopovich with a gesture.

GLAFIRA: I've been wandering about here and there, and went to investigate the kitchen. Just look, on a shelf, these twenty-nine little white china jars. (*She tips them out of the cloth and arranges them on the small round table.*) The tops are perforated and there's something written on them. Of course I don't speak foreign languages, but I licked each one – that's pepper, poppy, mustard, fennel; this is dill, vanilla, ground nuts, carraway, cinnamon. Well, of course, I grabbed the lot. They'll do fine. But I mustn't go on like this. Maikov, what am I to do with all my things? And then, just look, a lovely little pair of false teeth.

ANECHKA: You poor thing. I didn't know you hadn't any teeth. . .

GLAFIRA: Of course I've got teeth. But you never know what might happen. If not for myself, then I can always flog them. Hundreds of people ask for them in towns. And now look. I've discovered quite by chance that this isn't at all an ordinary kettle. Oh, Frau! That monster Hitler looks after his own. Put this kettle on the stove, and there's no need to watch it. All on its own, as soon as it starts to boil, it starts to whistle. Boy, does it whistle! As soon as I heard it whistle I said to myself – that's just what we need. But I mustn't go on like this. What am I to do with all my things? Where am I to stow my luggage? A most intricate kettle: I wouldn't mind a dozen of them. Staff Captain!

[14]

MAIKOV: Madam, with due respect to you and your family, I can't allocate more than three pairs of cart horses and two motor cars for your transport.

GLAFIRA: If the divisional commander orders you to, you'll do it. What does he give me? Three pairs of cart horses. Am I to lie down and die in this land of our enemies?

ANECHKA: You know, Glafira, you're a bit odd. You shouldn't attack the commander and the unit like this.

GALINA: I think Comrade Doctor, I'll go up to my room. I'll wait for you there. (*Moves towards the staircase.*)

GLAFIRA: Why? What's the matter?

ANECHKA: Nothing, nothing.

GALINA: To try on some clothes . . .

GLAFIRA: Who is trying on clothes? She is? There's no point, Galina. Her tiny size, her chest . . . Let her stay in her uniform. The major won't mind. But, have you a large selection?

Saliy – or is it Zamaliy? – one cannot tell them apart – comes running in through the door on the right, leaving it ajar. He is out of breath.

SALIY: It's the divisional commander! A major with him, and some fat lady lieutenant! (*He nods towards the door through which one now can see in the distance another large room.*)

MAIKOV (*in a rush*): Come on, my fairy princess! Remove your loot!

Glafira rapidly collects the jars into her cloth, and picks up the kettle. Saliy disappears. Galina comes to a halt on the first step of the staircase. Maikov issues his commands as if on the parade ground, but with a touch of humour:

Att-en-tion! To the right, dress! (*Marches off with a military step towards the piano, opens it.*) Musicians, quick march! (*Plays, while standing, Mozart's "Turkish Rondo".*)

There enter, to the strains of music, from the depths of the second large room a tall imposing Lieutenant-Colonel Berbenchuk, adorned with many medals, a ruby-cheeked, plump Major Vanin, and a very young Lieutenant Gridnev, whose prematurely puffy face is cherubic. Maikov stops playing, and with a sternness of voice suitable for the parade ground, but with the same touch of theatricality, announces:

Comrade Colonel! Permit me to report! Everything is ready for the celebratory dinner!

Berbenchuk pompously acknowledges the report, makes a gesture of "dismiss", moves forward and examines the mirror.

BERBENCHUK: A sumptuous spread. (*With emphasis*): No slaughtering of livestock?

MAIKOV: I let them live.

BERBENCHUK: And no harm to the civilians?

MAIKOV: Didn't find any.

BERBENCHUK (*looking at Gridnev*): In which case, I suppose we deserve this treat.

GRIDNEV: As Suvorov[4] used to say, what's won on the field of battle is sacred.

BERBENCHUK: Well said. And to the point. I must confess it would be a pity not to avail oneself of what's been won on the battlefied. May I present the accredited representative of Counter-Intelligence SMERSH, and Staff Captain.

MAIKOV: Maikov.

GRIDNEV: Gridnev.

They shake hands. Maikov pulls him along downstage, walking between Anechka and Glafira, who has frozen, still holding the cloth and the kettle.

MAIKOV: De-lighted. Delight-ed!

GRIDNEV: What are you delighted about?

MAIKOV: That our establishment is complete. Don't laugh at me, but I hate holes in establishments, as well as in trousers. No establishment is complete without its own SMERSH agent. So why not us? And here you are, sent to us. I love the SMERSH lot. We must establish close friendship and have a drink to start with. Now I would like to introduce our Medical Officer, the Divisional Doctor Grigoryeva.

GRIDNEV: Delighted. What do they say – a snake around the goblet?

ANECHKA: That's a witty beginning, but I'm at a loss – what snakes, which goblet?
She moves over to Vanin, her heels clicking firmly, and introduces him to Galina at the foot of the stairs.

MAIKOV (*nudging Gridnev in the ribs*): What's your first name then?

GRIDNEV: Vladimir.

MAIKOV: Vlad? Well, I'm Alex . . .

GRIDNEV: I don't quite follow . . .

MAIKOV: Stop being so fierce. You'll follow all right. That's the way I am, see? We're generous – there! (*Slaps him on the shoulder.*) My arrangements are fine. Everything will go swimmingly!

BERBENCHUK: Hmm, yes . . . This . . . actually . . . this is my wife. I've got Army permission for her to come with me.

GLAFIRA (*freeing one hand which she stretches out like a stick*): Glafira Berbenchuk.

GRIDNEV (*reserved in his greeting*): You've got Army permission, did you say?

BERBENCHUK: Yes, yes. I filed a special application. After all, I've been in the Army for twenty years, training, campaigns, let's face it.

GRIDNEV: I see. However, there are three women here. On our way here I thought you mentioned two . . .

BERBENCHUK: This third one . . . is . . .

GLAFIRA: A slave. Snatched from Hitler's claws . . .

MAIKOV: Hey, look at you! Taking quite an interest in skirts, I see . . .

GRIDNEV: Now, look here. You're getting a bit too familiar.

MAIKOV: Sorry, old chap. I'm a simple man. I want to have fun, to share my experiences, to open my heart. I hope you don't stick by the rules, Yes sir! No sir! May I be permitted to report, sir!

GALINA (*to Vanin*): No, no, just call me Galina.

GLAFIRA (*summoning Berbenchuk who is moving towards the group of people by the staircase*): Eugene, it's time to dress for dinner. (*Taking hold of him, she leads him to one of the doors.*)

GRIDNEV: Army regulations, taking account of our position, allow us . . .

MAIKOV: Not another word . . .

BERBENCHUK (*on his way out*): Captain Maikov.

MAIKOV: Here.

BERBENCHUK: Make arrangements for our guest.

MAIKOV: It's all been done.

BERBENCHUK: Supper in an hour?

MAIKOV: As you say, sir, An hour.

Exeunt Glafira and Berbenchuk.

MAIKOV (*to Gridnev*): I must dash to the kitchen, but just let me say one thing: you've touched a sore spot. A combatant soldier knows how to get out of bed at night; knows how to sound the alarm as fast as a fireman; knows his battle orders by heart and the unwritten code; he's part of the garrison; he's all discipline. Isn't that so?

GRIDNEV: I suppose so . . .

MAIKOV: Come on, say it. Isn't that so?

GRIDNEV: Yes, it is.

MAIKOV: Well, I'm doing you a favour, you idiot. I'm doing my best for you.

He leaves quickly, after Vanin and Anechka.

GRIDNEV: Miss!

Galina continues upstairs.

Miss!

Galina slows down.

GRIDNEV: One moment!

Galina stops at the top of the staircase; Gridnev is in the centre of the stage at the foot. During the rest of the act the electric light steadily fades, the stage growing darker and darker.

GRIDNEV: Come down here for a second.

GALINA: I'm in a hurry.

GRIDNEV: What are you in a hurry about?

GALINA: What is it you want?

GRIDNEV: I have this little business to discuss with you.

GALINA: I'm listening.

GRIDNEV: No, it's me who's going to do the listening. You'll be *telling*.

GALINA: What?

GRIDNEV: Come on down.

GALINA: I can hear you from here.

GRIDNEV: I don't want to shout.

GALINA: Shout? What right have you to shout?

GRIDNEV: This little purple book . . . (*pulls out his credentials*) do you know its power? (*He turns over the pages.*) Whoever presents this has a right . . . to detain civilians . . . to investigate . . . Do you know the limits of my rights? Come on then. Come down!

Galina descends a few steps.

More.

Galina descends a bit more.

More!

Galina is almost down.

Come here. I see you're nervous . . .

GALINA: The way you're behaving . . . (*She can hardly stand up, and leans on the mirror.*)

GRIDNEV: That's neither here nor there. Let's be precise. There's always a reason for being nervous. He whose conscience is clear before his Country isn't . . . Have you got some certificate, some German *pass*?

GALINA: No.

GRIDNEV: No? Why not? The Germans used to issue passes to our people. That's no secret.

GALINA: Not to us.

GRIDNEV: Who's us?

GALINA: Slave labour from the East.

GRIDNEV: Did they give you something instead?

GALINA: Oh, yes, a badge.

GRIDNEV: Yes, I know. I'm just having a little joke. You've unpicked your little badge very neatly: not a trace, no telltale mark, Miss er . . .

GALINA: Pavlova.

GRIDNEV: Wonderful, wonderful! Do you know, there was a philosopher in England, an agnostic, Hume. He used to say – don't trust your eyes.

GALINA: Can I go?

GRIDNEV: Yes, of course you can go.

Galina hurriedly ascends the first steps.

GRIDNEV: Let me ask you one more question.

Galina stops.

GRIDNEV: Where are you from?

GALINA: From Kharkov.

GRIDNEV: You don't say! So am I. I know every bit of Kharkov by heart. Even the houses and their numbers. Come on, give us a smile. It would be nice to remember our younger days ... The chances of war ... When were you liberated?

GALINA: When was I what?

GRIDNEV: I'm saying, when did they set you free?

GALINA: Oh, I see, *liberated.* Last night.

GRIDNEV: Where?

GALINA (*coming down*): Here.

GRIDNEV: So, you lived here?

GALINA: I did.

GRIDNEV: How long for?

GALINA: About a year. I can't remember exactly.

GRIDNEV: What were you doing here?

GALINA: I was a servant.

GRIDNEV: What kind? A cook? A milk-maid?

GALINA: No, a chambermaid.

GRIDNEV: But in Kursk, what did you do?

GALINA: In *Kharkov* I was a student.

GRIDNEV: A nice little place to spend the war in. One is tempted to say ... A starched apron, a lace collar. The master of the house – some grinning S.S. officer, so gentle in the family circle ...

GALINA: You know perfectly well, we were taken by force.

GRIDNEV: But it is *you* they chose. After all, you're not unique. Who was it you managed to please? The Nazis, or just men?

GALINA: But what was I to do?

GRIDNEV: You could have joined the army, the partisans. You could have been a Zoya Kosmodemyanskaya[5]. But not you, my little bird. You worked it all out perfectly. What you've forgotten is that we were going to come, that we *have* come! Just look out of the window. (*He goes to the window and pulls back the curtains.*)

Shimmering blue light floods the ball-room, where the light of the electric bulbs is already dim.

Have a look! The night is blue. Look how many headlights over the three autobahns! That's your death rolling in! That's fate delivering its avenging blow!

Galina has turned towards the window. She makes a momentary gesture of despair behind Gridnev's back.

GRIDNEV: And look at all those fires – one, two, three! (*He hits his chest with his fist.*) We risked our lives in front of the tanks. We sacrificed ourselves for our beloved Leader and our country. While you stayed here, curled up on a couch, book in hand. Have a look – the artillery, the motorised infantry, the cavalry! And do you imagine the glorious Intelligence of the Cheka will put on kid gloves for you? You thought you could sneak in under the protection of Stalin's sacred flag at the moment of victory. Didn't Mayakovsky[6] say: he who is not with us is against us? (*Advances on Galina. She moves away, and, tripping over a chair, sits down.*) Your entire life, your friends, your meetings, where you are from and why you stayed behind here all by yourself, our Intelligence network knows all about you in detail. We can see right through you! Come on, cards on the table. Your mask is off! (*He bangs on the table.*) You've lost!

Galina droops. A pause.

One thing could remove half your guilt in the eyes of the people: if you say you're sorry and make a clean breast of it.

Who gave you secret instructions? What was your assign-
ment here?

*At the last words Galina lifts her head in surprise, and a faint
smile lights up her face.*

GALINA: Oh, Lord! Such pitiless words, said in such threat-
ening tones. Do you like chocolates? I've always had a sweet
tooth. (*Rising.*) Let's pinch some while nobody's looking.
(*She takes a handful out of a dish and offers them to Gridnev.*) Do
have some with me. Don't worry, they're not poisoned! Ha,
you look terrified. Did you think I was left behind to offer
poison to Soviet officers? Never fear, these chocolates are
delicious: they melt in the mouth. (*She eats one.*) Well, I'll eat
it on my own, and like a faithful dog will die in agonies,
crawling towards the door. Won't you be sorry? Or would
you be pleased that your prognosis was perfectly correct?

GRIDNEV: Are you having me on?

GALINA: Oh, no, you're quite right. Everything you've said is
true. I am a woman born to be happy! I don't care what
country it's in, and under what idiotic government. I can't
stand uniforms. I prefer to wear a dress. I wouldn't exchange
fashionable shoes for an aircraft gunner's boots, nor my silk
stockings for a soldier's socks. Where did you get the idea
that I want to be free? I can be a slave if I want to. I want a
home and family. How could such brilliant minds imagine
that I want to drive a tractor? Maybe I was destined to be a
butterfly. Perhaps I was born to be a Geisha girl. You can
talk about equality for a hundred years, but you can have it as
far as I'm concerned. We used to have quite a good time
without it. What's all this rubbish – as if I owed something to
somebody all the time . . . I never took anything from
you . . . I've eaten three chocolates, and I'm still alive. Do try
one.

Gridnev hesitates.

Shame on you. Turning a lady down. And in any case what's
all this stuff in aid of? Why all this melodrama? You yourself
don't believe a word of it. People in smart uniforms like

[22]

yours don't throw themselves in front of tanks. Suppose, through some chance of war, you'd found yourself in Crete, I bet you'd have said: To hell with it all, and fallen in love with a Greek girl . . . Where am I from? From Kharkov? From Rovno? Did I lead a blameless life? Well, not quite. But am I guilty before the Soviet people just because I'm good-looking? Why, when you're so young as to be barely out of the spotty stage, are you so keen to become a spy? The way you talk – trumpets, curses, corpses – one day you'll be ashamed of all this nonsense!

GRIDNEV: Miss Pavlova, I hope I didn't . . .

GALINA (*walking round the table*): Didn't, kidn't, fidn't . . .

GRIDNEV (*following her*): Let's make friends.

GALINA (*offering her little finger*): My bones ache.

GRIDNEV: You're quite right of course, and I'm wrong. But I'm sorry, and being sorry . . .

GALINA: Removes half the guilt.

GRIDNEV: You must forgive me. In the line of duty I had to . . .

GALINA: You didn't have to anything. Don't you understand that?

GRIDNEV (*pursuing her*): Miss Pavlova: Which is your room?

GALINA: So that's it! All leading to that.

GRIDNEV: Yes, that's it. I'll not let you go . . . I love you.

GALINA: Don't use that word!

GRIDNEV: Galina, my darling, my sweetheart (*embracing her*).

GALINA (*tearing herself free*): Let go!

GRIDNEV: Only till morning.

GALINA: And after that?

GRIDNEV: After that I'll let you go behind the lines. I'll get you a pass, some papers. Or else, if you like, you can stay here, with me. You can travel with me. How about it?

GALINA: I don't see how . . .

GRIDNEV: We'll think of something. My secretary, say. Come on, Galina, my sweet, look at me. In wartime you can get away with anything. Who'll know?

[23]

Attempts to kiss her. Galina tears herself away.

GALINA (*raising her voice*): I'll scream.

GRIDNEV (*rooted to the spot*): All right then. Go on, scream. As one great Humanist put it – if the enemy does not submit, destroy it.

A pause. They stand apart.

Scream! Scream! As loud as you can. When your defenders come running . . . You must have been away from the Soviet Union for a long time. You don't know the meaning of this blue stripe. Let them come running. I only have to say: I have a-rres-ted her! That's all. After that you'll find yourself deserted. You'll be locked up in the cellar. Five days, no food, no sleep!

GALINA (*slumps*): So. A woman has only two choices: to be locked up in a cell, or to be a tart.

GRIDNEV (*approaching slowly*): Don't be so stubborn. You've nothing to lose. Just this one night. After that we'll go our separate ways. You can do what you like.

The bulbs are quite dim. The blue light through the windows grows ever more purple from the reflection of the fires. As it grows dark, the light from the forgotten candles becomes more noticeable. Saliy comes running in and stands to attention.

What do you want?

SALIY (*saluting*): Private Saliy, sir. I am to conduct you to your quarters.

GRIDNEV (*hesitating. To Galina*): I'll see you in your room . . . Just remember, there are guards at every exit and entrance.

He and Saliy go out. Galina walks over to the staircase, mounts a few steps, but comes down again. She wanders listlessly about the stage. She draws the curtains together, one after another. She sits at the piano, her head bent. Then she begins to play. While she is playing she doesn't notice that Captain Nerzhin has entered. He isn't wearing his greatcoat. He stops and listens, and then sits down silently. When Galina stops playing:

NERZHIN: Darf ich sie bitten, gnädiges Fräulein, ein bischen noch?

Galina jumps up. Nerzhin rises too. They look searchingly at each other.

GALINA: Sergei!!

NERZHIN: Galina!

They kiss briefly; touch hands rapidly; talk, interrupting each other.

I . . .

GALINA: I, too . . .

NERZHIN: Did you retreat with the Germans?

GALINA: Oh, dear. That's a long story . . . I don't recognise you. In your uniform! A captain! I went to study at the Vienna Conservatoire. To learn the piano.

NERZHIN: How do you mean – in Vienna?

GALINA: In Vienna, yes, which is haunted by the ghosts of Mozart, Haydn! But what about Liussia? I met her in the bomb shelter, just before the surrender of Rostov. She was as white as a sheet . . .

NERZHIN: She fled to the Caucasus. And then, further and further into the mountains, under fire, along goat tracks. She got to Kazakhstan, half dead. But do explain . . .

GALINA: Oh, Lord, there's so much to tell you, Sergei. (*Walking about restlessly.*) Where can we go? Come to my room . . . No, you can't do that.

NERZHIN: Why, what's the matter? What are you afraid of?

GALINA: You must be careful, too, if you have anything to do with me.

NERZHIN (*undoing the holster of his pistol*): Why, any Germans here?

GALINA: If that was all. Some half-baked Cheka type is prowling around.

NERZHIN: You must be dreaming. This is Staff H.Q. of our Unit.

GALINA: Aren't you afraid?

NERZHIN: Afraid? What of?

GALINA: Am I glad you're here. As soon as you go – where are

[25]

you going? You will take me with you? Please say you can – I beg of you!

NERZHIN: I don't understand . . .

GALINA: You'll understand soon enough.

NERZHIN: Of course I'll take you, but I'm going to the front . . .

GALINA: Which front?

NERZHIN: Does it matter to you?

GALINA: It's terribly important to me which front. Just give me a lift. I'll get off at some point and try to get there myself. Oh, Igor, Igor! This miracle proves you are right: God does exist, somewhere in Heaven.

NERZHIN (*looking round*): Who are you talking to? Who's Igor?

GALINA: My fiancé.

NERZHIN: Is he here?

GALINA: No, luckily not: he's not one of you.

NERZHIN: So he's with them?

GALINA: Yes, he's with us.

NERZHIN: I can't understand a word you're saying. Sit down and tell me all, in the proper order. You're getting married?

GALINA: Yes, I am. Wait a bit, I'll tell you everything. Look, I'm still shaking. He was interrogating me here . . .

NERZHIN: Who was?

GALINA: That Cheka type.

NERZHIN: What type?

GALINA: The type with horns.

NERZHIN: Calm down. You're now with me. What's more, here, close to the front, they've not got much power over us.

GALINA: You used to be such a weedy student, but look at you now – you're taller, harder. Your voice, your gestures, are so mature. They say the battle front is horrible, and yet it regenerates men, the way motherhood regenerates women. When are you leaving? Soon, I hope. I must escape, I must get away.

NERZHIN: What's the hurry? You're not among wild beasts.

GALINA: Almost.

NERZHIN: What's going on here. Has the mirror fallen down?

GALINA: They're having a celebration.

NERZHIN: But why are *you* here? How did you get to this place?

GALINA: Not all at once Comrade Captain. I hate the words "Comrade", "Citizen" . . . "Sir" or "Madam" are much more civilised. As for me, I'm a slave labourer, a servant, liberated yesterday, with the arrival of your army.

NERZHIN: Don't say that. How on earth did you get here from Vienna? Who's your fiancé? Why so silent, eh?

GALINA (*in some difficulty*): Your lot would think it a betrayal. He's your enemy. He's an officer in the Russian Liberation Army[7].

NERZHIN: Not necessarily.

GALINA: What?

NERZHIN: An enemy.

GALINA: Sergei, my love. Are you off your head? Then, why do you work for them? Are you one of us?

NERZHIN: Hold on: "one of us". Not to be an enemy doesn't mean being a friend.

GALINA: Well, tell me. There's a commissar here, Vanin. Is he a good man?

NERZHIN: None better.

GALINA: What about the political instructor?

NERZHIN: Not just him. They're all a splendid lot.

GALINA: If that's so, then tell me, how is it, by what chemistry, by what power, are you all made to serve these *Morlochs*, these enemies of our people?

NERZHIN: Serve whom?

GALINA: The *Morlochs*.

NERZHIN: Are they something out of H. G. Wells?

GALINA: No, out of Moscow. And their leader is from Gori.[8]

NERZHIN: *Morlochs!* I like that.

GALINA: Don't laugh. We've laughed our youth away, alas.

NERZHIN: "Alas", Galina. You're quite right. Your words remind me of how once, when I was a school-boy I was running along, carefree and whistling. An old man stopped me and said fiercely: "How dare you whistle, you puppy. We've whistled Russia away, with all this piping."

GALINA: That's not it, that's not it. You're still joking. I don't like it. You talk about all this as if it were someone else's tragedy. But look around you, just stop to think – do you know what sort of a place you're living in? We have an agreement, Igor and I, look. (*She pulls out something which hangs on a chain around her neck.*) This is a phial; it's instant poison, so that if he and I fail to meet, or if, God forbid, I fall into your hands, I would rather die than find myself in one of those prisons.

NERZHIN: Galina, are you quite mad?

GALINA: I've no wish to rot in prison; to choke on copper dust in Dzhezkazgan, or to bleed to death from scurvy in Zapoly-ariye; to search for food in dustbins, or to sell myself to the Ruler of Siberia!

NERZHIN: You're talking rubbish, Galina.

GALINA: That was our agreement. Don't talk me out of it; don't waste your breath. He'll shoot himself. No one will take him alive. The U.S.S.R.! It's impenetrable forest! A forest. It has no laws. All it has is power – power to arrest and torture, with or without laws. Denunciations, spies, filling in of forms, banquets and prizewinners, Magnitogorsk[9] and birch-bark shoes. A land of miracles! A land of worn-out, frightened, bedraggled people, while all those leaders on their rostrums . . . each one's a hog. The foreign tourists who see nothing but well organised collective farms, Potyomkin[10] style. The school-children who denounce their parents, like that boy Morozov. Behind black leather doors there are traps rather than rooms. Along the rivers Vycheg-da and Kama there are camps five times the size of France. Wherever you look you see epaulettes with that poisonous blue stripe; you see widows, whose husbands are still alive, who surreptitiously wipe away their tears; and you see all those invented *Matrosovs* and silly *Zoyas* who fulfil their plans one hundred per cent. Applause! For a land of miracles, where hymns and odes are sung to hunger and misfortune. For the miracles of Communism when whole peoples are transported into the depths of Siberia overnight. And Rokossovsky.[11] Wasn't it only yesterday that he was in a labour camp, a slave, not a man at all, felling trees in Siberia, loading them on to barges, but who, today, is summoned, he is needed, he's made a Marshal. But tomorrow, perhaps he'll be back in Siberia. Oh, I can't bear it . . .

NERZHIN: Galina, my dear, you frighten me. It's you, and yet it's not you. Your face shines with a new light. You're possessed. Your eyes burn. Who inspired all this? Where does it come from?

GALINA: As your komsomol girls would say: I'm forged anew. But they, they are like pack horses. It's true, they know their lot. They must haul till they die. There's no escape. Yet we've all been forged by the same blacksmith on the same black anvil.

NERZHIN: I do agree with a lot of what you say. Most of it is true. But nothing is all black in nature.

GALINA: Don't argue. I don't know. All I do know is that I shall be dead tomorrow unless you take me away today!
Nerzhin is bemused by all he has heard.
Tell me, how am I to behave among the Soviet people? Is there some special way? Can you advise me?

NERZHIN: You'll manage. We're a rough lot, of course. All you have to do is to laugh, to sparkle, to slow foxtrot around!

GALINA: We . . . we don't seem to know each other.

NERZHIN: That's true. Let's just say there was a time when I thought I was in love with you. So who's your fiancé? A White Russian?

GALINA: No, he's like you and me – he was a Soviet, a lieutenant. He was taken prisoner.

NERZHIN: And in the German army . . .

GALINA: No, it's Russian army now; you're out of date. They have Russian armies and Air Force as well.

NERZHIN: So I've been told.

GALINA: You have been told?

NERZHIN: That they established a committee in Prague.

GALINA: He told me. He was there. Oh, it will be splendid.

NERZHIN: Galina, darling, it's too late.

GALINA: It's a bit too late.

NERZHIN: Not just a bit, Galina . . .

GALINA: What a wet blanket you are. You always imagine the worst. But life isn't just a logical progression. We must have our dreams. There's a need for tenderness, Sergei, my dear . . . I have only one option open to me. When you write to Liussia, tell her that quite by chance you were the one to lead her friend to the altar. The candles were burning; Scriabin's music played; but the bride wore black, and it seemed oddly in keeping. Tell her you weren't destined to meet the groom: that you never entered the church where the wedding was to take place. But Sergei, I may be hard-hearted, fickle, bad, but do wish me joy . . . (*sobbing*).

NERZHIN: Galina, dearest. What now? I told you I would take you away. In a day or two you'll . . .

GALINA: I've stopped. I cried because my heart was so full. You arrived like a descending angel and will disappear again, perhaps forever . . . I was so close to him! But the tanks! Your tanks got in the way. I must tell you that Europe trembled that terrible morning of January 13th when the last gates of Warsaw fell to the hammer blows of Ivan the Mighty. A Walpurgis night of confusion: a witches' sabbath. Some were stunned; some sneaked away; some ran; while I — I made a dash here in the hope of getting to Rastenburg where his legion is stationed; where he is; where my life is either to end or to start again.

NERZHIN: So that's where he is! I should have guessed.

GALINA: Why, what do you know?

NERZHIN: I . . . I don't know anything.

GALINA: But you just said . . .

[30]

NERZHIN: I understand now how you ended up here. Come on, my love, tell me more.

GALINA: That's all. It took me ten days from Vienna. There were fires, bombs, always changing trains, complete confusion. And now that I'm almost there, when I could have got there on foot, your lot turn up, God knows from where. They're like menacing lava, these armies, these endless armies . . . You look worried – what is it?

NERZHIN: It's that we've got Prussia in a pincer movement, and that any minute now, the pincers will close.

GALINA: And he's there!

NERZHIN: Yes, he's there.

GALINA: The Germans were talking about it, but I refused to believe it. But it's written on every face I've seen. Well, let it be . . . so long as I can be with him and we can die together.

NERZHIN: Galina, darling, hold your head up high. You'll never win if you let your spirits droop. If you're to face the gallows, march under a different banner. I don't know the man you've chosen, but if he's worthy of your love, tell him I've no fears for the fate of Russia while there are women like you. No matter that for the time being we wear different brands on our foreheads, that we sport different uniforms. I give you my word that in a couple of days you'll be over the other side, whatever my marching orders – West, North, or East.

GALINA: Shake!

NERZHIN: Shake!

GALINA: What a weight off my shoulders. And again (*They clasp hand, crosswise*). There's no turning back. Hurrah! Would you mind if I kissed you once more?

NERZHIN: I would not.

They kiss. Suddenly the lights go up. They gasp and jump apart.

GALINA: I told you it was a miracle. (*She runs happily to the piano and starts playing.*)

ACT TWO

The same scene, the same actors, in the same position. Enter Berbenchuk, unnoticed by the other two. He walks slowly towards them, listening.

BERBENCHUK: So you're responsible for the music!

GALINA (*rising shyly*): Comrade Colonel . . .

NERZHIN: Comrade Colonel: I came at your request . . .

Berbenchuk makes a friendly gesture, as if to say – we are off duty. Throughout the next scene he is very gracious, his bass voice undulating.

BERBENCHUK: I too, I also used to play. (*Sits down at the piano and executes a few bars of Chopsticks.*) Well, what do you think of my battalion commander? He's not a lady's man, a bit out of touch with all these . . . niceties. Compared to other officers, he's a bit eccentric, a theoriser. But don't imagine it's easy to be a commander. (*He sits down with Galina at the little round table. Nerzhin is a little further off.*) They sit around in the staff room, bored to death, yet they have to be on the alert. If there's no fighting, they immediately send representatives to Berbenchuk. So then, with the paymaster's help, we give them lunch, and the trouble is over. Otherwise, they demand to be given a unit, to be sent to the front, whether you like it or not. So I have to consider where to send them. After all, there are only three batteries. But I'm not easily rattled. I take the bull by the horns. I ask – what is your special interest? Well, this and that. Fine. You want to look after the technical side? You're interested in pushing paper around? Secret papers? Fine. You'll be attached to Makarov. He's in charge. Keeps order. Army stores? Every little bit is labelled: "Private So-and-So is responsible". Should you be interested in the stores re-

[32]

cords – here they are for you to read, neatly written out in copper-plate – four files. As to our operational maps, well, each one's an ikon. A hundred transparent sheets, so fine one daren't touch them. Makarov is a stern taskmaster. Yes, we regular soldiers deserve respect. Now, that other fellow, Likharyov, he's a bit flighty. Loves dancing. He's here today. He's one of those who never wait to hear the end of an order. Yes, sir, certainly sir, and he's off, straight into a minefield. But out he comes, unscathed. In an ordinary field of potatoes he comes a cropper. (*Roars with laughter: Galina smiles politely.*) He rushes into battle; likes his drink, and is quite hot on girls, if I may say so. His men would follow him anywhere; plunge over ditches; squeeze through minute crevices – if there's a granary in sight! Their stores are full to bursting, the whitest of white flour. Or else they'll kill a pig, out of sheer pity, seeing as how the poor thing was hurt by a splinter on the battlefield. (*Laughs.*)

GALINA (*innocently*): With a gun?

BERBENCHUK: Mmm, yes. But once it's skinned, how can you prove anything? Let me finish. Any inspection of his set-up I do myself. I wouldn't dream of allowing inspectors anywhere near it. Ye-es. But whenever a bespectacled intellectual arrives from Moscow, to find out if our technical reconnaissance is at a high scientific level, he's directed to Nerzhin. Humidity needs adjusting? Gra-da-tions, and all that? We're not country bumpkins. And what's the other thing? Temperature? . . .

NERZHIN: Inversions?

BERBENCHUK: So the fellow's as pleased as punch. (*Berbenchuk kisses his fingers.*) But when an instructor from the Politburo arrives, then I see at once that something's up. A denunciation! Trouble! So he, too, is despatched to Nerzhin. And he'll be so blinded by science there, he won't know if he's coming or going. In Nerzhin's section even a nit-wit can manage to look down his nose and pontificate on lease-lend, or on Churchill, or what have you. He (*nodding towards*

[33]

Nerzhin) is hardly human. When everybody's drunk, he isn't. When everyone's asleep, he's awake. He's reached the rank of Captain, and he still looks down on the way we do things here. He's softened up a bit lately, though, I'm glad to see. He's married, and is sickeningly faithful to his wife. Faithful beyond measure.

GALINA: Is there a measure to faithfulness?

BERBENCHUK: Well, you know, where an officer is concerned . . . Having arrived at Headquarters for his instruction, he . . . and you . . . should have . . .

NERZHIN: Made music?

BERBENCHUK: That's fine, my dear chap, but war doesn't wait. Out there, there is bloodshed, casualties every second . . .

(Having noticed Saliy/Zamaliy who enters, carrying a bowl.)
    This way Saliy!

NERZHIN: *(gets up with determination and unfolds a map from his folder.)* Can I have your instructions, sir?

BERBENCHUK: *(to Galina)*: Californian raisins. Spoils of war. Have some.

NERZHIN *(advancing)*: Instructions, please, sir.

BERBENCHUK: Wait!

GALINA *(taking some raisins)*: You're having a very cosy war.

NERZHIN: I request . . .

BERBENCHUK: Don't pester!

GALINA: But where did you get . . .

BERBENCHUK: There were some Red Cross stores around here. I was able to discover precisely where, and we pounced . . . Do you smoke? *(Getting a packet of cigarettes from one of his pockets.)* These are Chesterfields, and these *(getting them out of another)* are Camels. *(Lighting one.)* Miss Pavlova, how would you react to the idea of being made a member of my Division?

GALINA: Can it be done?

BERBENCHUK: You name it: I can do it. The Division is mine, so is the rubber stamp. I can order a new uniform; or

[34]

have a fashionable skirt run up in no time. Just think how patriotic that is: an extra uniform to defend us. And *personally* I would be very pleased . . .

GALINA: But in what way can I be useful to you?

BERBENCHUK: Not to me, not to me, Miss Pavlova, but to the *country*. You just watch: I issue an order, and you are enlisted forthwith. Simple as that.

Maikov enters swiftly, accompanied by two soldiers.

MAIKOV: Where's the milk? American milk?

The under-cook points to it on the table.

And the German?

(The cook points.)

Dried? Condensed? (*Admiring the table.*) Hell's teeth!

BERBENCHUK (*good-humouredly*): Hey, Maikov.

MAIKOV (*absently*): Yes. (*To the under-cook*) And what's this?

BERBENCHUK: Hey . . .

MAIKOV: What are these peasant mugs doing here?

BERBENCHUK (*irritated*): Staff Captain!

MAIKOV: Yes . . (*to the under-cook and soldier*): Take them away, you idiots. (*It is only at this point that he bumps into Nerzhin and greets him casually as he walks on.*)

BERBENCHUK (*thunderously*): Staff Captain!

MAIKOV: Yes sir. (*In an undertone to the soldiers*): Crystal glasses, thin ones, the ones that ring!

BERBENCHUK (*Beside himself*): Staff Captain!!!

MAIKOV (*freezing to "attention"*): I'm all ears, sir.

BERBENCHUK: Do I have to repeat myself?

A pause. Maikov's attitude, as if forever frozen into complete submission, disperses the Colonel's doubts. He is mollified.

Would you make this lady citizen – I don't know if she is a Miss or a Mrs – a soldier of our Division, as of this date. She has agreed.

NERZHIN (*rising, formally*): Comrade Colonel, I . . .

GALINA: Agreed? When?

BERBENCHUK: Is that clear?

MAIKOV: Yes sir.

BERBENCHUK: Do it then!

MAIKOV (*resignedly*): I can't.

BERBENCHUK: You can't?

MAIKOV: We have no right. And, alas, even *you* . . .

BERBENCHUK: What's that? If she's taken in at my command . . . Do what is necessary; make it formal. After all, who am I? I'm the Supreme Commander.

Maikov looks meaningfully at Berbenchuk, who wilts.

But if that's my wish . . . If you . . . If I . . . You know better how to tackle this.

MAIKOV (*rattling it off*): Instruction zero-zero-one hundred and eighty-nine, Order four hundred and fifteen states that without the clearance of the Regional Army Committee, or the certificate of the Medical Committee . . .

BERBENCHUK: But what are you for? Aren't you the Staff Captain? Well, do it somehow or other . . .

NERZHIN: Comrade Colonel, I must insist on my instructions . . .

MAIKOV (*approaching Berbenchuk, quietly*): Especially now that we have this fellow from SMERSH . . .

BERBENCHUK (*to Nerzhin*): Ah, yes, your instructions. Come over here. (*Moves away with him.*)

Galina, trying to move away unnoticed, goes past and ascends the staircase. Nerzhin has opened a folder of maps and holds one in front of Berbenchuk.

Where's the map? Ah, here . . . The enemy have retreated to the East. They are entrenched, entrenched . . . Where the hell is Liebstadt? Where is it? Eh? It was here . . . Or is it to the side? Well, anyway, the enemy have retreated; we are advancing; there are battles going on (*he makes sweeping gestures over the map*) here somewhere . . . or perhaps here . . . I will even venture a guess that we've got as far as the frontier.

NERZHIN: I would like to be precisely sure. You showed me first . . .

Berbenchuk is not looking at the map, but over it at Galina, who is

*leaving. Nerzhin grows silent. A sergeant comes running through
the door on the right. He is in winter clothes, with a sprinkling of
snow on his coat.*

SERGEANT: Comrade Captain, our cook, who is in the
Opel . . .

MAIKOV: What about him?

SERGEANT: He's stuck.

MAIKOV: Not with the cake?

SERGEANT: He can't get out: he's holding the cake in both
hands.

Galina has gone. Berbenchuk hurriedly returns to the map.

BERBENCHUK: So . . . that's the situation – in general.

MAIKOV: Get a detachment to pull him out! What the hell!

SERGEANT: Who shall I get, sir?

MAIKOV: Telephonists, signalmen, scribblers, topographers,
radio-operators!

The sergeant runs off.

NERZHIN: I didn't quite get it . . .

BERBENCHUK: You'll sort it out. You're clever enough. Cap-
tain Maikov will give it to you in detail.

*He dismisses Nerzhin by touching the peak of his cap, and hastens
after Galina. Nerzhin, still holding the folder of maps follows
Berbenchuk with his eyes.*

MAIKOV (*looking at Nerzhin, sings*): He who marks out his
destined route on a torn map is rather cute . . . (*He puts his
arm around Nerzhin's shoulders and turns him towards the
mirror.*) Not bad, eh? What do you think? After all, we're
bound to remember a day like this! King Arthur used to
entertain at the round table, but who had a meal on a mirror?
Such a celebration will be remembered a long time.

NERZHIN: But what's the reason for it?

MAIKOV: Two: the Major's birthday, and . . .

NERZHIN: And?

MAIKOV: Oh, any old thing.

NERZHIN: Look, while you're still sober, give me my instruc-
tions.

Nerzhin moves the little table forward, spreads the map over it; they both sit down, Maikov cross-legged.

MAIKOV: Now, then. The situation. As usual, nobody knows what the situation is. You hear a rifle shot, and you turn the motorcade to the right. Then you investigate. Not bad. Liebstadt. The Passarge. Over the bridge to the right shore, and – nach Osten!

NERZHIN: To the East! But wait! (*Jumping up*): That means Prussia is . . .? (*An excited handshake.*)

MAIKOV: Done for! Our tank corps has finally broken through today: cut through the Germans at Elbing, and broken out to the Baltic!

NERZHIN (*in great excitement*): That's what Samsonov[12] always dreamt of!

MAIKOV: And that's the second reason for our celebrations. N. brigade will fix up a telephone-line for you. You're to do your reconnaissance in this (*he marks it up on the map*) sector. Pass your information on to us by radio, or else use the brigade. Your job is to find them. You must be ready by 0400 hours. Where's your battery?

NERZHIN: When I was leaving, they were setting off.

MAIKOV: So you have an hour or two to stay with us. You'll be able to appreciate our elaborate repast and entertainment. I'd be very hurt if a connoisseur like you, Sergei, didn't . . . Everything was going so well – a happy birthday, the war coming to an end, the appearance of this charming girl – but then in crawled this reptile from SMERSH.

NERZHIN: Who's that?

MAIKOV: Haven't you met him? Sent by the Army.

NERZHIN: Accredited?

MAIKOV: Of course.

NERZHIN: Not a front-line soldier?

MAIKOV: Well, what do you think? A pink piglet, stuffed full of the rubbish of the N.K.V.D. school. The whole world begins and ends with his school: how were you dressed; what did you eat; how to sniff people out with tracker dogs . . . I must go. Just cook up some report and sketch out a plan. Mark it 4 a.m.

NERZHIN: But where is the front; where am I to go, Alex? I've no idea.

MAIKOV: Just write something. As Vanin says, all one needs is a piece of paper. You give it to me; I pass it on to the Army, and the Army will despatch it to the front. That way you can stay the night. No need to go anywhere. Write some nonsense – who's to know? They've hundreds and thousands of bits of paper like that. If I find out something new in the morning, I'll add a correction or two. If not, I'll send it as it is. That's no problem!

NERZHIN: No, but it's silly.

MAIKOV (*drawing himself up*): Is that so? Then may I add, Comrade Captain, that I shall be expecting the messenger with your report and plan by 5 a.m.

NERZHIN: Where shall I send him? Here?

MAIKOV: Of course.

NERZHIN: That's sillier still. He won't manage to get either here or to Liebstadt by 6 even.

MAIKOV: That's nothing to me. You ought to know. You're an officer, not a child. That's why the intelligence units are nicknamed 'the eyes and the ears of the Army' – intelligence in general and the artillery in particular. (*As Maikov proceeds to wax lyrical, Nerzhin looks at him with amused admiration.*) Now that we're in the land of the enemy, surrounded by hostile forces, our attitude must be especially disciplined, our reports especially precise, as never before . . .

NERZHIN (*hums*):
>Having discovered rebellion on board
>He pulled a gun from his belt
>(*together*)
>Scattering golden flakes
>From his lace-embroidered cuffs.

MAIKOV: Just write something! (*Exit.*)

Nerzhin, alone, sketches, writes and talks to himself the while.

NERZHIN: Who'd have believed, innocent and trusting as I was in 1940, I would now be sitting down meekly falsifying historical evidence, and concocting this sort of rubbish . . .?

Vanin enters, smoking a pipe. Every time he appears he smokes something different – a foreign cigarette, or a Russian one, or a gypsy-like self-rolled cigar of incredible proportions. Nerzhin doesn't notice him.

NERZHIN: When we were young, did we imagine this war to defend the Revolution would turn out like this – labels and tags and bits of paper to deceive our superiors? Heroic sacrifices – they're all pie in the sky. Everything we're told is so unlike what happens in fact.

VANIN: What a surprise! Education doesn't improve the mind. You should read little and write even less.

NERZHIN (*jumping up*): Comrade Major, they tell me that today . . . Congratulations! Many happy returns, with all my heart. (*They shake hands.*)

VANIN: Many thanks, old chap. But I'm getting old. It's time I retired.

NERZHIN: But how old are you?

VANIN: Thirty-six.

NERZHIN: Is that all? I'm nearly that. But all the same, my muscles, my arteries . . .

VANIN: How old are *you*?

NERZHIN: Twenty-seven.

VANIN: Ha! Wait till you get to my age.

NERZHIN: Nine years' difference is nothing.

VANIN: The point is it's my fourth decade. I'm aware that life's been wasted; that there're no curly-headed kids under my feet.

NERZHIN: Kids?

VANIN: Yes, kids: happy, healthy kids. We bachelors, who eat in canteens and sleep any-old-where, there's something missing.

NERZHIN: That's just it: *canteens*. They remind me of my

childhood, the menu scribbled with chalk on a scratched blackboard. And it was always the same: cabbage and tapioca pudding. But look at you: well built, rosy cheeked: perhaps not too much military bearing, but still an army gloss. No, you're not too old.

VANIN: To look at, perhaps, but I feel old. When I came to town from my village during the heady days of the New Economic Plan I was only a boy. And ever since then I've been in a whirl . . . ever since. Those were the days!

NERZHIN: Yes, I remember!

VANIN: You? Remember? Bread, threepence a loaf, and cinema hoardings the size of a house. But we tightened our belts and went into battle, thinking that we were storming the sun itself: that the smell of meadows would permeate the towns; that villages would glisten with shining glass laboratories; that four hours of dedicated work would be enough to achieve equality; that we would become masters over life, over nature, over history. After our voluntary Saturday shifts we took part in discussions; after cell meetings, we worked in clubs; after factory work we attended universities. All duly authorised of course. Amidst all this activity, dear boy, I failed to notice that my life was passing by. And now that I'm almost forty, with a scar from a wound at Khortitsa, a scar that's more jagged than Chkalov's flight . . .

NERZHIN: The unrepeatable Five Year Plan. It flourished under our own skies. And it was you who . . . (*He pretends to throttle himself.*)

Vanin goes towards the radiogram and switches it on absent-mindedly. We hear: "The news about the latest, grandiose victories of the Red Army stirred a flood of enthusiasm and unprecedented patriotism among the women textile workers in Ivanov. At their numerous shop-floor meetings the women workers drink toasts to the wise strategies of genius, the leader, father, teacher and best friend of the textile workers, Comrade Stalin. The women spinners of Molomonov and Natyagushin stayed by their forty looms for

72 hours, urgently fulfilling the plan for 1969 . . ." Vanin switches the radio off.

VANIN: Ah, well. We know that our sleigh is wonky. But the disgruntled mare goes on pulling it up and down hill all the same.

NERZHIN: All that's happened, Major, could have been a bit gentler – without executions, without the terror. Ever since that decisive quarrel between Bukharin[13] and Stalin . . .

VANIN: But there was no quarrel. The first was writing innumerable memos; the second was placing his supporters in key positions.

NERZHIN: So that's how it was.

VANIN: Yes, that's how it was.

NERZHIN: So much the worse! Since historical truth is hidden, and since it's being further obscured, the opposition from the right . . .

VANIN: What opposition? From the left, from the right – all that, you know, is just words, my dear fellow. What are you trying to find out from me? You know what I think. All Bukharin wanted was that Russia should have enough food. He was right, therefore.

NERZHIN: That's just what I think. He was right. I feel sometimes that the very core of the Revolution, its very structure had a fatal flaw. But where and in what way? I scratch about for the truth, like a pig digging for truffles.

VANIN: So did I. But now, I fear, things are much simpler.

NERZHIN: Tell me how?

VANIN: Why do you want to know?

NERZHIN: It's of the utmost importance to me!

VANIN: I said 'simpler': I should have said 'more complicated'. It would take too long, and this isn't the place. You would want statistics, graphs, diagrams, and I'm not versed in these things. You're clever, of course, but can you make a distinction between words and facts?

NERZHIN: Er . . . in what way?

VANIN: Oh, dear! Just go away and die! You've answered it

already: you don't know the distinction. No amount of books will make you understand. Imagine a collective farm so prosperous that even our book illustrators couldn't portray it: where great lorries, and not your miserable hand carts, overflow with the daily harvest of grain; where there are milking machines, motorised ploughs, electric grain driers; where everything is ordered and planned; where – don't laugh – not a penny of the communal money finds its way into private pockets; where there are orchards, bee-hives and vegetable gardens; where the hostel is a colonnaded house, and where some old codger sits issuing coupons for everything from apples to appartments. There's discipline, naturally, and time-keeping – after all, the enterprise is worth millions, order must prevail. In the office the schedule is being worked out for the following day: who goes where; who does what. Now then, would you say a peasant would want to join this collective farm paradise?

NERZHIN: I would say, yes.

VANIN: Well, let me tell you, he would not. Imagine being told that someone was coming into your study to break down the wall between you and the next door study, because in there there are other thinkers like yourself, and intellectual efforts must be pooled. The District Committee would be issuing the topics for research, and your timetable would be worked out so as to insulate you from distractions like visitors or parties! Would you accept that?

NERZHIN: Of course not. To lose the freedom of ideas . . .

VANIN: There you are then. Is a peasant a cow? How does he spend his years, months, days? Thinking of his stomach? He dreams of his harvest, working in the sun-drenched fields. He loves his little apple tree, not only because it provides him with fruit. Do you see my point? Points such as these make up the whole of life, my friend: millions of them. Otherwise you're welcome to sit down and reel off laws on the subject of class struggle. Just as the distinguishing features in a police dossier can't provide a convincing photofit, so a Marxist method can't explain or evaluate or improve society. Marx, of course, was right in many things, but to start an explosion, to hold this live wire with bare hands . . ! You could, I suppose, imagine that the grizzly bear is a bone-setter, and self-taught at that.

NERZHIN: Good God! Stop heaping coals upon my head. I expected all sorts of things, but not a blow below the belt. Tell me, though, how come you carry your rank and your duties as a commissar so easily, so lightly?

VANIN: Me? Oh, I'm guided by some vague precepts. I let myself be carried along by the current. The main thing is, I can't see, and I don't know, anything better. I am a bell which summons people to church, but stays outside it . . .

NERZHIN (*walks about agitated*): But how's one to live? What's one to think?

VANIN: Thinking is the last thing you want to do. There is authority. There are orders. No one grows fat from thinking. You'll get your fingers burnt from thinking. The less you know, the better you sleep. When ordered to turn the steering wheel, you turn it. Suppose tomorrow they tell you the earth is square? Well? What do you do? You know the situation is awkward, but you go to a party meeting and declare: "Comrades, the earth is square." Do you know the story about a political adviser who is asked by the soldiers: "How come we must respect the Church again?" And he says: "Well, lads, I was all wrong. I used to say: there is no God, but, blow me, now there is . . ." (*They both laugh.*)
Maikov enters quickly. Saliy and Zamaliy follow him carrying a huge cake. A tall dark cook overtakes them, mincing fussily along. He wears a white cap and a crumpled, unbuttoned army coat over his white apron.

MAIKOV: I'll lock you up in a dungeon, you freak. Squashing a cake like that . . . Put it there (*showing where. Saliy and Zamaliy put it ceremoniously on the table.*)

COOK: Comrade Major!

MAIKOV: I've been a captain for two years, and nobody has

[44]

promoted me to major yet. Where did you steal those ten
skirts? Why were you late? Why are you always drunk?
Shame on you! Into the dungeon with you, you ruffian. Any
questions? Straw and water.

COOK: Many years of devoted service. How can you, Com-
rade Captain!

MAIKOV: If I had time, I swear by all that's sacred, I would go
into the dungeon myself, out of sheer curiosity. Oh, ancient
stones of medieval prisons, where so many noble hearts
beat . . .

COOK: I defended my country with my very blood . . .

MAIKOV: And what about those pigs you slaughtered . . . and
the sheep you shot? Arrest him!

Saliy and Zamaliy throw themselves on the Cook.

COOK (*fighting to free himself*): Stop it, you louts. Go easy.

MAIKOV: I'll get a woman cook tomorrow – young and
neat . . . Ugh, you swine! One cook died in bombing;
another stumbled on a mine; the third drowned; good
people never survive. And look at you – you were poisoned,
burnt; you fell off a rock; and you are still alive.

COOK: O.K., lock me up, but I shall die innocent.

MAIKOV (*to Saliy and Zamaliy*): Don't make a mistake, mind.
There's a wine cellar next to it.

VANIN (*stopping them. To the Cook*): It was because of you that
we were investigated four times by the political department.
And you are still in one piece.

MAIKOV: I quarrelled with the Corps Commander of 35th
Division because of you. And you are still alive.

COOK (*freeing himself, insolently*): Because of me? You've got to
prove it, thanks very much (*takes off his cap*). It's not my fault
that I happened to tame a colt which looked very much like
one the Corps Commander lost . . . Anyway, today I've
baked a cake so light that nobody in the whole Army could do
it better. I'm proud of it. May I (*looking at Vanin*) go? *Vanin
waves his hand. The cook, free now, departs with Saliy and
Zamaliy.*

[45]

MAIKOV: I'd have punished him.

VANIN: Ah, to hell. So far as looting goes, he's not as flagrant as some. But, joking apart: a secret order to the Front, Number 007 (*as if reading*): "It has been observed that when units of the Second Byelorussian Division crossed into Prussia, they were responsible, with the connivance of officers, for the, so far occasional, incidents of arson, killing, rape, theft and pillage both in villages and along the roads. It is the duty – more, the right – of all those in command to stop these acts forthwith in their own units, as well as in any others without distinction, by any means, including execution, in order to maintain the honour of the Soviet Army."

NERZHIN (*whistles*): That's rough! But what are we to do about the instruction of the Politburo about "our sacred revenge"? What about those *parcels?* What about those pamphlets entitled "Russian Reckoning with the Enemy"?

MAIKOV: F-friends, do tell me for God's sake, does that mean I can get rid of Glafira's transport?

NERZHIN: No, but really it's a bit much. First, you egg old Tommy Atkins on and promise him the earth. While he's needed you entice him to march to the Baltic ...

MAIKOV: Are you telling me that we're not to drink liqueurs; have pastry without vanilla; eat dried potatoes? No, something's wrong here. It will surely all be explained ...

NERZHIN: You promise him half the world as you're preparing for the leap ...

MAIKOV: A victory without a celebration – that's too much.

NERZHIN: Are we just rosy innocents, wearing epaulettes and singing hymns?

MAIKOV (*looking out of the window where the light is no longer blue but crimson. He closes the curtains*): Rape, yes, rape is terrible, but if the little German girl is, as they say, *willing* ...

NERZHIN: That soldier, who cowered with me in the marshes of Ilmen as we were being strafed by German fighters, am I to execute him? Just because he pinched a "Mozer" watch? Or, even dragged a girl into a bunker? Lying there with him in the Russian cornfields, and saying good-bye to life in the middle of scorching smells and smoke, holding him down and saying "Don't move, this one isn't for us" – am I to raise my hand against him now? Before our offensive, didn't you issue an order which was the exact opposite, and didn't you justify that too?

VANIN: What if I did?

NERZHIN: Where's the truth then, where are the lies? You used to say that however much the soldier suffers, at the end of the road there will be prizes . . . And now, am I to shoot him?

VANIN: Just you try! I'd have you court-martialled at once.

NERZHIN: So what about the order?

VANIN: What's an order? (*He blows.*) A piece of paper. When a thing like that begins to move, there's no stopping it. Do you think, O lowly insect, you can control events? As to the order, comply somewhat, but not too severely, and don't contravene it either. Learn to be less rigid. Our little lives are overrun with great and dirty politics. (*Embracing both Maikov and Nerzhin.*) We do, dear friends, torture ourselves far too much with doubts and decisions. But regardless of us, everything is for the best.

NERZHIN: The Major is fond of saying: "All's for the best"; "Too much learning will not improve the mind"; "Fear not the beginning, fear the end". I can't get to the bottom of these sayings.

MAIKOV: What the devil do you mean, it's for the best? There we were living quietly, peacefully, as if under the protection of our guardian angel, and blow me, if that fat, pink piglet from SMERSH doesn't burst in to disturb our peace.

NERZHIN: There he goes, torturing a nice girl . . .

VANIN: What, already?

MAIKOV: He interferes in everything; gets in the way . . .

VANIN: He won't get far here. He came, and he'll go again.

MAIKOV: What makes you say that? Everywhere else, these plenipotentiaries get entrenched like a bloody carbuncle. Do you think we're so special that he'll just stay a week or a month and then be off and leave us in peace?

NERZHIN: According to Gauss[14] (*shrugs*) some elliptic function: an exception to the rule.

VANIN: Gauss, my foot. I knew how to get rid of those carbuncles.

NERZHIN: MAIKOV (*together*): You did? How?

NERZHIN: What did you do?

VANIN: I would quietly collect evidence against them. There he would sit, the wretched creature, behind locked doors, writing away. (*Furiously*): Vermin, and so young too. I can see right through them, for all their uniforms. Little fleas serve bigger fleas, but they can all feel threatened by a piece of paper.

MAIKOV: But what did you put on it?

VANIN: Oh, anything, whatever came into my head. The main thing was to be ahead of them; to prevent them getting a head-start. This one let on about a secret installation, in his cups; another one gave false information when filling in his form; the third expressed doubts about our victory; the fourth was sympathetic to the enemy – anyway I can't remember it all. But once you've put it down the whole thing snowballs. They devour each other like rats. They're both vigilant and suspicious. Some bald-headed investigator will look into the doings of a curly-headed colleague and will find him guilty of this, if not of that. After all, everyone is guilty if you look closely enough. In 1937, for five months, I could not go to bed properly because of *them*, listening for footsteps on the stairs, for the knock. Late at night, when everybody had locked their doors, my old mother would say: "What's going to happen, Arseniy? What do they want? To lock everybody up, so that only *they* remain?" She would wander about

[48]

making the signs of the cross over all the shutters and doors with her feeble, wrinkled hand . . . Not a night would go by without some arrest being made, those vermin darting in and out. They arrested all the big-wigs and their children, party leaders, trade-union leaders, the bourgeoisie and the proletariat, big and small, but there I was, intact, shivering on my leather couch. All that remained in town was the Chief of the G.P.U. and me, Arseniy Vanin. I was all prepared to tell them everything and sign anything, like a lamb led to slaughter, about who my connections were from my very childhood. I tidied up my affairs, but, there, they never took me – I survived!

MAIKOV: As for me, being an artist, the favourite of Muses, I was nearly done for. (*The eyes of the other two are turned towards him. Maikov sits, relaxed, on the edge of the mirror, dangling his legs.*) Some clever dick once suggested that in the design of posters, note-books, exercise books, in paintings, in sculpture, in everything that's been touched by a brush, a chisel or a pencil, there lurk agitation, subversion, sabotage. Searching, detecting, endlessly till they dropped, they espied Trotsky's goatee beard among oak leaves; an inscription "Down with the CP(b)" on Prince Oleg's shield. Nowadays, of course, I'm an Impressionist, but then I belonged to the narrow-minded realist school. At the end of my studies, for my final diploma, I presented a carving entitled "The Kiss of Psyche and Eros". It was rather realistic and somewhat lacking in modesty. Between ourselves, when people gather roses, they assume certain poses. (*He jumps down and tries to represent his sculpture, becoming either Psyche or Eros.*) She's leaning back, one arm hanging down: he is holding her by her waist, leaning over her like that! Well, some dolt of a Komsomol detected a Swastika in it. No diploma, naturally, and I was dragged here and there to the Party Committee. All the gymnastics of detection were applied to my miserable creation – learned experts, a commission – to determine if it was indeed a Swastika. They had several juries. Had I known I wouldn't have touched mythology – to Hades with it! On one occasion the Director himself crouched before Psyche and Eros in various positions, staring. I couldn't restrain myself any longer I was so furious, and shouted from the hall, "Why don't you get under the table, you might get a better view of it." So they decided at once that a Swastika it was and that my sculpted pair should be examined by the N.K.V.D.

VANIN: Hey-ho, that was a cheerful year. One story after another. A friend of mine, a vet, got arrested. They said: "You've been unmasked; you're an enemy of the people; confess that you were poisoning livestock." But, says he, sitting on the edge of his chair, trembling: "There was no cattle plague this year." "Ah-ha, you would have liked there to have been?" And they knocked his teeth out. They locked him up in a cellar for a week under a lamp so big (*he demonstrates with both hands the size of the globe*); three-hundred grams of bread was all he was given; not allowed to sleep – as soon as he fell asleep, they'd wake him up: "Write down, I poisoned . . ." "The collective farm camel." "Insolent, are you? Making fun of the Cheka?" They gave him a beating. "Go on, confess, you rat. Otherwise we'll send you to that famous place where ninety-nine men weep, while one man laughs." He became so weak that he confessed. However, still having his wits about him, he stated that he used to inject cattle against glanders. They immediately increased his bread and soup ration, but condemned him to the North for fifteen years, ten solitary. Well, when the days of Yezhov[15] were over, someone came across his forgotten file. It pays, sometimes, to invent a clever lie. Horses suffer from glanders, not cattle. Yes, they got the message in the end. He shared his cell with an old codger, a simple peasant in an old caftan and birch-bark shoes – good old Russia. He never lived to see his trial. To get some peace, the poor old thing testified that he was plotting a rebellion on his farm; that he had a tank, eleven hand-grenades and a number of shot-guns; that he had planned to attack Leningrad, raping the Komsomol girls all the way . . . In those days the Military College of the Supreme Court churned out two hundred sentences a day. It happened like this: two guards would come running in: "Are you Petrov?" "I am." (Or Petushkov – they muddled things up a bit). All would remain standing: no time to sit down. All done ship-shape and naval fashion, Whistle and lift, Loading, Heave-ho, ten-twenty. Or else, it would happen like this. A load of unsentenced deportees would arrive North from Chelyabinsk. They would be chased into the yard to hear their verdicts. An officer would come out, wearing elegant boots, followed by a sergeant with case-files of Mishkins, Mandrykins, Gromovs, all this in the middle of a cruel winter. They would stand, huddled, stamping their feet, moving around in a circle. In this temperature it's impossible to turn the pages over with bare hands. So, not to torture himself and all the others, the officer would announce: "Your verdicts are ten years – eight years for some. Is that clear? Dismiss. Be off in to your bunks" . . . *A pause.*

Well, Maikov, why are you silent? Cheer us up. Fetch your guitar.

Exit Maikov. Nerzhin is rigid with tension.

NERZHIN: Then what they used to say is true? About tortures, torments?

VANIN: So . . .

NERZHIN: That they used to beat, harass, starve, chase people out naked into the snow; that they squeezed a dozen people into a single cell . . .

VANIN: There was a time when . . . when, at dawn, they would push people into the cells who had been imprisoned under the Tsar. The events were so confusing for them, their plight so miserable that they would rush towards any newcomer asking: "Whose revolution now? Who is in power? Tell us quick, comrades!"

Re-enter Maikov.

MAIKOV (*singing and strumming on his guitar*):

> The golden rims of the Alpujarras
> Are growing dark and dim.
> At the sound of my guitar
> Come out, my love, be seen.

VANIN: I don't think that's a very cheerful song: there are better ones . . .

MAIKOV: Which one would you like?

VANIN: Well, Alex, the one about the steppe beyond the Volga, about the steppe . . .

They sing together.

> Far, far beyond the Volga the wide steppes spread,
> Where freedom grew and flourished like a tree.
> Think how bitter was the life men in those days led,
> For a man to leave his hearth,
> His native village and his wife,
> And go beyond the Volga to be free.

The accompaniment has stopped, but Vanin goes on singing, with a sob in his voice:

> . . . For a man to leave his hearth,
> His native village and his wife,
> And go beyond the Volga to be free.

ACT THREE

The same scene, the same actors, in the same positions. Glafira, dressed for dinner, descends the staircase.

GLAFIRA: Staff Captain! Captain! The Commander said one hour, but two have gone by . . . (*Noticing Vanin, lowers her voice.*) Excuse me, Major.
Vanin and Nerzhin continue to sit motionless. Maikov, irritated, bangs the guitar strings, rises, thinks for a moment, then claps his hands three times.

MAIKOV: Saliy and Zamaliy!
Saliy and Zamaliy rush in simultaneously, one from the left, the other from the right.

SALIY AND ZAMALIY: Yes, sir!

MAIKOV (*indicating the banqueting table*): Let's mount an assault on this redoubtable spread. Summon the guests! (*Gives Glafira a nudge with the guitar.*) Have fun, my girl! And the roast piglet is to be here in five minutes; after that, in seven minutes, let's have the meat-ball conserve. (*He claps his hands again; Saliy and Zamaliy dance around the stage as if in a ballet. To Glafira*):
What are the views of this member of the Military Council?

GLAFIRA (*imitating a somewhat vulgar gypsy style of dancing, stamping her feet, playing the guitar and singing in a fast tempo*):
> Play, my guitar, play and ring out,
> Sing, gypsy, sing me such a song
> That will obliterate my poisoned days,
> Days without peace or love.

Saliy and Zamaliy are gone. As soon as Glafira's last note dies down, Maikov puts a foxtrot on the radiogram, turns up the volume, and leads Glafira. She holds him with the back of the guitar. From the corridor Likharyov and two girls in military uniform rush in, performing a complicated dance in a threesome. They are Katya, who is tall, free-and-easy, her military shirt unbuttoned at the collar showing a white vest underneath, and Olya, a shy blonde. In comes the Head of the Chemical Unit who circles rhythmically around the dancing threesome; he is bald, elderly and portly. Likharyov offers him Katya, so that there are now three pairs of dancers, whirling about wildly to compensate for the small number dancing. In the meantime Vanin has pulled himself together; he walks slowly over to the radiogram and switches off the music. They all stop. Glafira examines the girls; they look at her. Nerzhin continues sitting in the same place.

VANIN (*to Nerzhin*): You understand, don't you. I gave permission for a small supper, a sort of family affair, but look at this – a ball.

MAIKOV (*looking around*): And non-political, as well.

GLAFIRA: Who gave Likharyov permission . . .

LIKHARYOV: Forgive me, Comrade Major. I knew there was a shortage of girls, and if I couldn't find . . .

MAIKOV: Nobody could!

LIKHARYOV: I couldn't invite the German girls.

MAIKOV: No patriot could!

LIKHARYOV: So I rush off in search, and what do I see? A familiar Chevrolet. And there is the Staff Captain of a unit I know. In terms of battle experience we are brothers, in a sense. We have a sister in commom.

VANIN: He's your brother? Well, get him!

MAIKOV: What a pig you are!

LIKHARYOV: No, you don't understand. We have a nursing sister in common.

KATYA: You are a wretch, Arkadiy.

LIKHARYOV: So I rush up to him: Help, Comrade! Now, he's the sort that will always come to one's aid. Katya, the typist (*he introduces her to Vanin*) is rented out for twenty-four hours, the way they rent them for a film project. "Take her, you're welcome." "What? Only one? You must be joking. I

[54]

need three, minimum two." "There aren't any more." But I spot a pair of blue eyes. "What about this one?" "Well . . . she's undergoing sniper training." "On a course?" "No, by herself." "Well, I give my word as an officer: all she'll be doing is drinking tea: no wine, upon my word."

GLAFIRA: How can you make such promises in advance, on a woman's behalf?

VANIN: What's more, you danced.

LIKHARYOV: Permission to speak – a foxtrot. I talked him into it: Olya shall come for an hour, no more. (*He introduces her to Vanin.*) She'll have to go beddy-byes early.

VANIN: Where're you from?

OLYA: From Vologda.

VANIN: Called up?

OLYA: No, I volunteered. I'm a Komsomol.

VANIN: My dear child, did you think we couldn't manage without you? You should be spending your time day-dreaming over books, or walking in the park. Oh, carefree youth, where art though gone?

MAIKOV: And how many Germans have you killed?

OLYA: Oh, dear. No. I've not taken any part in battles yet.

The Head of the Chemical Unit examines the table and is trying to engage Nerzhin in conversation.

HEAD OF CHEMICAL UNIT: How much longer are we going to damage our health by abstaining?

PARTY ORGANISER (*enters with Gridnev*): Outwardly, it's National, but the content is Socialist. Isn't that so?

GRIDNEV (*constrained*): I suppose so.

PARTY ORGANISER: So that our duty to the Party . . .

They cross the stage. Berbenchuk enters from the left. He wears his ceremonial uniform and is beaming. Maikov attempts to begin his report, in a rather affected manner.

MAIKOV: Comrade Colonel . . .

BERBENCHUK (*stops him good-humouredly*): My first question is, where do these girls come from?

[55]

LIKHARYOV (*pushing Katya forward*): Due to an emergency (*pushing Olya*) from the rear reserves.

They shake hands. Saliy and Zamaliy enter carrying roast sucking pig on large dishes. Thereafter they serve at table. Maikov, from time to time, gives orders to both of them and to other soldiers.

PARTY ORGANISER: All this will be discussed by the Party Committee.

Galina appears at the very top of the staircase; she wears an evening dress. Anechka is quite transformed by a pretty dress and new hair style. Gridnev is the first to notice them and rushes forward to greet Galina.

GRIDNEV: Yes, yes, we'll discuss it later, Secretary.

KATYA (*to Berbenchuk*): I've heard this one before, Divisional Commander!

HEAD OF THE CHEMICAL UNIT: Well, Nerzhin, do you think we'll ever start to eat?

PARTY ORGANISER: This dish, is it real silver?

GLAFIRA: What are we waiting for, Eugene? We're all here.

BERBENCHUK (*having also spotted Galina and approaching her slowly*): What do you mean, *all*? Look at them coming down, so lovely in their party dresses!

GLAFIRA (*rushing to overtake him*): Oh, Anechka, what a ludicrous bow!

Berbenchuk, being held back by her, is slow in reaching Galina, who is approached by Gridnev.

GRIDNEV (*familiarly*): Where've you been? I went up to see you.

GALINA (*with dignity*): Comrade Lieutenant . . .

GRIDNEV: Did you forget?

He attempts to take her arm. They are separated by Nerzhin, who squeezes himself between them.)

NERZHIN: Excuse me. (*Offers Galina his arm.*) May I?

Galina takes his arm. Gridnev stands in the way.

GRIDNEV: Who are *you*?

NERZHIN: And who are *you*?

GRIDNEV: No, *you*?

NERZHIN: I'm a battalion commander, but *you?*
In the meantime, Berbenchuk reaches Galina and stealthily leads her away. Upstage there is some pre-banquet animation. Gridnev and Nerzhin are downstage.

GRIDNEV (*attempting to reach Galina*): Hullo, there. Where're you going?

NERZHIN (*standing in his way*): All right then, who *are* you?

GRIDNEV (*trying to get round him*): None of your business.

NERZHIN: The business may not be mine, but the girl isn't yours.

GRIDNEV: Trying to be clever, are we?

NERZHIN: Not clever, and not daft, either.

GRIDNEV: A sight too familiar.

NERZHIN: I give as good as I get.

GRIDNEV (*fixing him with his eyes, emphatically*): So, what sort of a person are you, Comrade Captain?

NERZHIN: A battalion commander, as I said.

GRIDNEV: I'm talking about your *origins.*

NERZHIN: I beg your pardon?

GRIDNEV: I repeat, your origins.

NERZHIN: You were asking . . .

GRIDNEV: I was asking who your parents, and your grand-parents, were, and you seemed to avoid my eyes.

NERZHIN: Well, no one's asked a question like that for a good ten years, and if one never expected to hear it again, how is one to react?

GRIDNEV: So you've heard the question before?

NERZHIN: Who hasn't? At every turn. But it's gone out of fashion. We're just Russians, just patriots.

GRIDNEV: You seem to be aware of this new formula.

BERBENCHUK: Comrades, please don't stand on ceremony: make yourselves at home. Come and sit down, sit down!

LIKHARYOV: Olya, darling, over here!

OLYA: I'm superstitious; I don't want to sit on a corner.
They arrange themselves around the mirror. Maikov walks towards Gridnev and Nerzhin.

GRIDNEV: Yes, things change. They move along. We're all just Russians again now, but with a difference. When you were applying for officer training, didn't you notice such a question in your application form?

NERZHIN: I did. I just thought it was an out-of-date form.

GRIDNEV: Special Departments don't have out-dated forms.

Maikov leads them to the table and settles them down: Gridnev is placed next to Glafira, Nerzhin next to Maikov himself. Prokopovich arrives at the last minute and squeezes himself on to an end, without a companion to talk to. We can hear the noise of eating and general conversation:

May I?

Please do!

A piece of ham?

What on earth is this?

No rank pulling.

This is Prussian pork, with good old Russian horseradish.

OLYA: I don't understand. When do you people fight? Ever since I arrived you've been doing nothing but eat, while back at home they're thinking of you, grieving over you, listening to the latest news.

When you get married, tell your husband . . .

Pour me some more . . .

Yes, but don't give me any fat . . .

So who will start?

The commander, who else?

Attention!

Silence!

BERBENCHUK (*rising*): I've been in command of this Division now for three years. Perhaps it's changed a bit since I took over, but we swept aside the enemy artillery fire. Perhaps the guns weren't always ours, but we have a right to claim that it was due to our counter-intelligence that we made this advance, this great advance . . . from Holy Moscow, and even from Rzhev . . . like a, like a flood . . . like some awesome lava, carrying our noble Soviet ideals . . . knowing no rest . . . always in the forefront of battle . . . under the same leadership – I've been here from the start, my deputy came later – at Staraya, at Oryol, at Bobruisk, at Byelostok. And so, today, to sum it up, we're active participants, not on the side lines. Today, is the Major's birthday, my deputy. He's not a regular soldier; he's not a combatant, but he knows where he belongs. And, what is more, even Prussia is down the drain . . . so it's appropriate . . . I'm a simple soldier, unaccustomed to . . . In short, I propose a toast . . . Ye-es, a toast, to the Army . . . to us . . . to . . .

GRIDNEV: Funny. There is a long established Soviet tradition which demands that the first toast is proposed to Him, who . . .

VANIN (*interrupting, holding up his glass*): who illuminates our path by the light of the red stars of the Kremlin. What do we mean when we say "the Army"? We mean the Supreme Commander! The Colonel is proposing a toast to Stalin!

Party Organiser applauds loudly.

BERBENCHUK (*with a hiccup*): Y-e-s, yes. Naturally. Yes!

All rise, clink glasses, rhubarb, rhubarb . . .

MAIKOV: We did have some liqueur somewhere. Bring it here, Saliy. (*To Gridnev*): Drink, like a man! In tumblers, Russian fashion, with or without *zakuski*. (*He fills Gridnev's and Nerzhin's glasses.*) Now the three of us are faithful friends.

He and Gridnev drink; Nerzhin hardly touches it. Maikov walks away.

GRIDNEV: So, what was your answer?

NERZHIN: Answer?

GRIDNEV: On your application form.

NERZHIN: Oh, that. A clerk's son.

GRIDNEV: Meaning?

NERZHIN: Meaning that my mother worked as a clerk in an office.

GRIDNEV: Not a complete answer. It doesn't give me a full

picture of you. And, then, who was her father? And your father? And finally, your father's father?

NERZHIN: Well, my father was killed six months before I was born. So what am I to say about my origins?

GRIDNEV: I'll help find the right pigeon-hole for you. Who killed him? Whose bullet? Whose shrapnel?

NERZHIN: German.

GRIDNEV: In the Army?

NERZHIN: Yes, the Russian Army.

GRIDNEV: The Tsar's Army.

NERZHIN: No, the Russian Army.

GRIDNEV: Shall we simply say a butcher's army?

BERBENCHUK (*animated, talking to Galina*): A huge crowd, you see, shouting, carrying things. So he rolls back a bit and then runs his tank straight into the store! (*Roars with laughter.*)

GRIDNEV: So what was he? The unknown soldier? I doubt it. His rank? Could your memory dredge up ...

NERZHIN: It could. A simple ensign.

GRIDNEV: Ah-ha. An en-sign. How come?

NERZHIN: Easy. He'd been a student.

GRIDNEV: Ah, a student. One moment. (*Lights a cigarette, importantly.*) He was the son of ...

NERZHIN: A peasant.

GRIDNEV: A Lomonosov?[16] You see traps are laid by those little insignificant questions. I see it all clearly now. Your grandfather was never a peasant. Where did your father get his money for studying? An income from a wooden plough? (*Nerzhin is upset.*) Ha, ha, ha. I'm only joking, Captain. You can breathe freely – for the time being.

BERBENCHUK: The tank is stuck; the engine is roaring; and out there a hospital is on fire. So he thinks the mob will loot the lot. He jumps up onto the tank turret and shouts: Hey, you infantry, leave something for me!

Galina laughs with Berbenchuk. Glafira is getting nervous. Maikov returns.

MAIKOV (*to Gridnev*): When did you start smoking? Recently?

GRIDNEV: No, long ago.

MAIKOV: Come on, stop pretending.

GRIDNEV: Let me tell you. It was when I was at college. I got drunk, and was after a girl, and suddenly there was that patrol. But they didn't arrest me.

LIKHARYOV (*to Olya*): I wonder what kind of a sniper you'll make. Just imagine what it's like to have a gun pointing at you.

GLAFIRA (*to Gridnev, pointing at Galina*): See that bit of skirt over there (*whispering into his ear*). She may have been a chambermaid, but she's a tart. Once I'd discovered that, I wasn't surprised that she ... (*whispers*).

GRIDNEV: You don't say!

GLAFIRA: Slept with the Nazis. Not surprising.

GRIDNEV: Such a lovely girl – and tainted.

GLAFIRA: Aren't you an innocent.

HEAD OF THE CHEMICAL UNIT (*to Katya*): How can one know? When I said good-bye to peace, I thought that that would be the end of my film-making. But the war's nearly over. I'm about to go back, and here (*he points to his chest*) I have a star; (*to his shoulder*) and here three more; while here (*pointing to his breast pocket*) a Party card.

ZAMALIY (*comes running in*): Sir ...

MAIKOV: Bring them in, bring them in! (*Zamaliy runs off.*)

HEAD OF THE CHEMICAL UNIT: I must say, once you have a medal, you breathe more freely.

GRIDNEV: Do you know, I almost went to bed ...

GLAFIRA: God forbid! It's the pretty ones that pass it on.

HEAD OF CHEMICAL UNIT: The next thing is to exchange a forty-year old wife for two of twenty, da-de-da, and life would be fine.

KATYA: Would *I* suit?

HEAD OF CHEMICAL UNIT: Tut-tut! A wife must not be thrown about: she's not a ball. Would you like some of this?

LIKHARYOV: I remember meeting five girls: they were as

young as you. They marched with a proud step, wearing medals. The medals of four of them were battle honours, but the fifth one was for "outstanding courage". "How did you earn this highest award?" I asked. She lifted up her pretty head and said: "I stood up to them."

Saliy and Zamaliy remove glass jars quickly out of buckets of boiling water and empty the meatballs onto plates.

GRIDNEV: Those bloody Germans have learned how to make home preserves?

HEAD OF CHEMICAL UNIT: First you fry them properly . . .

GLAFIRA: And while they're still hot, you seal them in jars and store them in the cellar . . .

MAIKOV: And leaving all this behind, the peaceable population has to flee . . .

LIKHARYOV: In come the barbarous Slavs . . .

ANECHKA: Who throw these jars into boiling water . . .

KATYA: They then remove the rubber rings, and . . .

NERZHIN: Here they are sizzling, as if straight from a frying pan.

MAIKOV: We'll have some frothing champagne . . .

PARTY ORGANISER: Or else ordinary Russian vodka . . .

GALINA: To quench our thirst
                We still demand
                A goblet full
                Of sparkling wine.

MAIKOV (*clinking glasses with Gridnev and Nerzhin*): No questions asked!

HEAD OF CHEMICAL UNIT: *I* want to ask a question: why no more speeches?

BERBENCHUK: Captain: that's an oversight.

NERZHIN (*rising*): Comrades, to maintain the tradition . . . But, being a soldier, I'll be brief.

Silence reigns.

When this commotion is over, when we have parted and gone our various ways, those of us who survive will long remember Major Vanin's special gift of combining gaiety with sadness and with firmness of purpose. We will remember that he was wiser than any of us, that he was . . .

PARTY ORGANISER: Devoted to the ideals of Lenin.

NERZHIN: That he distinguished between the dead letter and the living spirit . . .

PARTY ORGANISER: That he adhered to the directives of the Political Wing.

NERZHIN: That he adhered and acted upon them with zeal. That he was both a politician and a man. Comrades, raise your glasses. Let's wish him a long life and a better one!
They all rise and drink. Rhubarb, rhubarb . . . To convey the next stage of general inebriation, the remarks that follow are spoken in a sing-song.

BERBENCHUK: Whom shall we appoint to be in charge of radio?
Arkadiy
Arkadiy
Who can compete with him?

LIKHARYOV (*dances his way to the radiogram*): The Russian soldier will now engage in battle with gramophone records (*he switches on*) foxtrot for the blondes: tango for the brunettes.
Soft dance music continues throughout the next scene. The following remarks are spoken, as if inwardly.

GALINA: I love to see the kaleidoscope of fate.

NERZHIN: I love to see the flow of unbridled festivities.

HEAD OF CHEMICAL UNIT: I love to hear the tinkle of crystal glass.

MAIKOV: Although your wings are tired, you still want to fly upwards.

ANECHKA: When in the midst of drunken stupor, you still have faith, you still believe . . .

VANIN: . . . that wasted lives will change for the better.
Thereafter in ordinary conversational manner.

KATYA: I see no point in worrying about difficult problems.

PARTY ORGANISER (*stretches his arm in the direction of*

Gridnev, his index finger pointing, like a figure on a poster): Are
your denunciations to the Party in order?

GRIDNEV (*grumbling, half-audibly*): Mind who you put your
questions to. God, what fools they send us.

OLYA: All right, if it's Tokay, just a sip.

MAIKOV (*to Gridnev*): We've so far had five Party Organisers,
each one dafter than the last.

GLAFIRA (*to Olya*): I sent my mother a trunk-full from Homel.

HEAD OF CHEMICAL UNIT: Could you pass that bottle, old
chap?

GLAFIRA: I send one parcel after another: this way we've
collected a trousseau for my daughter.

MAIKOV: Hey, let's sing a drunken song.

GRIDNEV: Ho-ho!

LIKHARYOV: Ha-ha!

BERBENCHUK: Well, Maikov?

MAIKOV: What?

BERBENCHUK: Say something . . .
A Toast.
A Story.
A Funny Story.

MAIKOV (*rising heavily. As he begins to speak, the music slows
down as on a run-down gramophone, and finally it stops.*)
Since it's my turn, I'll try and say something suitable for the
occasion.
Silence.
I'm in a funny mood today. You're expecting some light-
hearted after-dinner speech, some jokes . . . But, dear
friends, it is today that I suddenly realised what these four
years of fighting mean to me. Victory is here – give me your
hand. I feel its soft touch: it's fragrant and gentle. But the
hand that held us down in the trenches – how hard it was!
Whoever forgets 1941, I'll scratch one of his eyes out!!
Everyone shudders.
And he who speaks evil of it – I'll scratch out the other. I
speak these burning words for all those who've been forgot-

ten, whose names are lost . . . When Messerschmitts flew over the fields of rye stubble, chasing every car, every soldier, we scrabbled in the dry dust of our roads, our lips parched. I see our Russia through tears, through flaming hay ricks, through fallen bridges, through smoke . . . Do you know what I'm proud of? Not that I'm among the victors, but that I was among those who retreated. When we were surrounded, we saved our guns, dragging them with ropes a few yards at a time, our muscles bulging with the strain. Of all the medals I'm proudest of it's this (*he touches his chest*) early, simple one. I'd give the entire collection for this little one (*he touches it*). I'm also proud of the fact that one of my forefathers fought against the Pretender. We were taught history not from Pokrovsky's text-book but from abridged extracts, specially selected, where a roll-call of saints consisted of the Razins, Khalturins, Bakunins and Dombrovskys; where Suvorov was described as an executioner, Kutuzov a lackey and Nakhimov a pirate. It seems funny now. But which of us, when filling in our forms, shunned our officer origins like the plague, and said that in our youth we were miners; that our fathers and grandfathers were peasants, and our great-grandfathers shepherds? I'm proud of the fact that the Dobrokhotovs fought at Poltava; that one of them was executed for treachery by Biron; that we fought at Rymnik and Preussische-Elau; that my great-grandfather Maikov is buried at Balaklava; that my grandfather took Plevna; that my father was wounded at Muckden . . .

He is still speaking as the curtain comes down.

ACT FOUR

The same scene; the same actors. There are now a samovar and tea-cups on the table. Some time has passed, so that a number of people have left the table and are dancing. Nerzhin is dancing with Galina; the Party Organiser with Anechka; Berbenchuk with Olya; Likharyov with Katya, and Head of the Chemical Unit with Glafira. General inebriation is in the air. Prokopovich is alone, with a bottle for company. Berbenchuk, still in ceremonial uniform, has a shiny black top-hat on his head. The radiogram plays a waltz loudly. To the right, at the little round table, sits Vanin. At the back, behind the mirror, more or less centrally, is Gridnev. Whenever a pair of dancers approaches Vanin, he takes the opportunity of teasing them.

VANIN: Sergei, look out! I'll be writing to your wife. Look out, Sergei.

NERZHIN: Don't single me out, Comrade Major. Everybody else is dancing. Why pick on me? Ah, well. There's nothing for it: go on, write away.

VANIN: Arkadiy! You cheat! What are your promises worth? Look, just look, Olya is dancing a waltz!

LIKHARYOV: It wasn't me. It's the Colonel. What can I do in front of a superior officer?

In the meantime, Maikov, unobserved by the dancing couples, smuggles in under the piano two photographers, who crawl out, the first setting his camera, the second carrying a flash. Maikov walks over to the radiogram and switches over from the music to the newscast. The music stops, and simultaneously there is the flash of the bulb. All are frozen as if in a dumb show, and listen in amazement to the announcer's voice: . . . "The leader of the whole of progressive humanity, the greatest of thinkers who ever lived, the genius and the wisest of men, powerfully per . . ." Maikov switches back to music, just as unexpectedly. Everyone starts dancing again, laughing at this prank. Gridnev is gloomy. The waltz speeds up towards the end and stops. Berbenchuk, waving his top-hat, dances with abandon a hopak across the stage.

BERBENCHUK: Having eaten
        Cherry cakes
        (*repeats*)

Laughter, applause. The dancing pairs walk about the stage.

LIKHARYOV (*approaches Nerzhin*): Excuse me, Signor, time's up. The lady's promised me the next dance. (*Takes Galina away to choose another record.*)

Nerzhin, left alone, wanders off to join Vanin and sits down next to him. Maikov sits down next to Gridnev.

HEAD OF THE CHEMICAL UNIT (*walking past with Glafira*): This (*pointing to his medal*) I have. And this (*pointing to his epaulette*) I have; and this, too (*pulling out his Party card from his pocket*). What's more, I have something in my savings book, and a few expensive coats stashed away in my suitcase.

BERBENCHUK: Saliy, over here!

VANIN: That's not Saliy, that's Zamaliy.

BERBENCHUK: Oh, hell. They've been here three years, and I still can't tell the devils apart.

Zamaliy comes running, carrying a bonbonniere. Berbenchuk offers sweetmeats to Olya.

PARTY ORGANISER (*walks past with Anechka*): That's the way it was, Doctor. But now, no sooner do I eat something than I have a cramp, here, and here, like this ...

ANECHKA: You *are* a cheerful partner. Come and see me later, and I'll give you some tablets.

MAIKOV (*to Gridnev*): So you took me seriously, did you? Don't worry. I'm a shy little man. My father, it's true, used to peddle pastries, but all the others looked after sheep.

NERZHIN (*to Vanin*): Where did you get this idea that "education doesn't improve the mind"?

VANIN: My friend, he who understands this needs no explanation, but he who doesn't will never see.

MAIKOV: To tell the truth, I'm a proletarian through and through – the illegitimate son of a servant girl. You did learn at school about the gentry, about how, if a girl got caught in the hay-loft . . . That damned feudalism. Le droit de Seigneur!

GRIDNEV: I see, but still, you're half noble by blood.

MAIKOV: Don't pay attention to blood. Look deeper. Deep down I'm a peasant, a worker. Yes, I'm proud of my rough origins: we, the Dobrokhotovs – that means "well-wishers", we wished well, but to whom? To the people, of course!

A tango. Galina and Likharyov are dancing. The music gradually dies down.

VANIN (*to Nerzhin*): I feel I'm responsible for everything. It was my fault entirely. Just consider: it was I who surrendered Lutsk, and Lvov. It was I who surrendered Novograd. At Kovel, I almost died, but no sooner was I better, than I surrendered Korosten. It was also I who surrendered Zhitomir. And later on, when no one was looking, during the general exodus, it was the two of us – Vlasov[17] and I, who gave in at Kiev.

MAIKOV (*to Gridnev*): But you did study the practical side of things?

GRIDNEV: Of course, both theory and practice. You must know how to proceed when making an arrest. There are millions of ways of doing it. It has to be done quietly. So that no one should know. You can disguise yourself as a pilot, an electrician, a chauffeur, a postman . . . For example, how do you arrest an archimandrite? Well, you ask permission to spend the night in his monastery.

VANIN: I surrendered Poltava, and Lubny and Khorol. As to all those Piryatins and Byela Tserkovs . . . It's a good thing that our lot never got as far as the Volga, otherwise we might have surrendered Stalingrad itself. As we started to fall back, no amount of rearguard defence, or of official order No. 227 or whatever, could stop us. I remember people saying:

"Friends, isn't Moscow behind us?" While I – while all of us – felt "To hell with it".

Anechka approaches Vanin and Nerzhin, who soon moves away, looks behind the curtains through the windows, opens his folder of maps, wandering about nervously. Galina, having finished dancing with Likharyov, talks to him and to Berbenchuk, while watching Nerzhin anxiously. Nerzhin goes out through the door on the right.

GRIDNEV: The archimandrite, of course, is only too happy to take in Christian pilgrims. The Cheka agents sit there, talking of the Last Judgment, and of Paradise. When the monks have gone to bed, the agents stand up and say: "You're under arrest, you vermin." Don't remind me of it . . .

GLAFIRA (*among a group of people on the left of the stage, sings to her guitar*):

> You can forget me, gypsies,
> I'm leaving the encampment.
> I am singing my very last song.

HEAD OF THE CHEMICAL UNIT (*very drunk, leaning over the bannister of the staircase, recites either to Katya, who is close by, or to no one in particular*):

> And I dreamt that my heart aches no more,
> That it's a china bell in golden Cathay . . .

KATYA: What's all this?

HEAD OF THE CHEMICAL UNIT: That's by Vertinsky,[18] Katya. Did you ever hear him sing?

KATYA: That old stuff. It's old . . . it's cloying.

She moves away. The Head of the Chemical Unit remains standing for a while, then comes down to the first step of the stairs. The music is quiet, as if from behind glass.

ANECHKA: Did you enjoy the party?

VANIN: I did.

ANECHKA: Why look so sad, then?

VANIN: Which of us can control his feelings? When the war ends, let's go somewhere far away, far from visitors, books, newspapers, news, from meetings and duties. Somewhere where the peasants are, beyond Tambov, Ryazan . . . You can be a doctor there, so long as you don't inflict too much damage. I'll be looking after an orchard, and seeing to the beehives. In the mornings a chill will rise from the river. Geese, flocks, silence.

ANECHKA: What fantasies! You'd be the first to get restless.

Berbenchuk takes Galina by the arm and leads her downstage, away from her group of people.

BERBENCHUK: Miss Pavlova, I'm bewitched. I'm charmed. I'm not that old!

GRIDNEV (*watching him; to Maikov*): So one can be arrested when one least expects it, least knows. Now that's a first-class arrest! When he's hurrying to an assignation, or off on holiday, or some new assignment . . . When he's away from his usual surroundings, his friends . . .

MAIKOV (*filling Gridnev's and his own glasses*): Oh, wine! Who is that nameless genius, lost in the mists of history . . .

GLAFIRA: Eugene!

Watching Berbenchuk anxiously, she has left her group. Berbenchuk's talk with Galina is animated. They have moved closer to Vanin. Anechka has walked over to the dancing couples.

MAIKOV: . . . who trod the grapes for the first time with his bare feet . . .

GLAFIRA (*from a distance*): Eugene, come over here.

BERBENCHUK: Well what is it now? (*to Galina*): Excuse me. I'm sorry.

LIKHARYOV: I used to love picnics, strutting around like a peacock, half my present weight.

Galina, left alone, looks uncertainly around.

VANIN: You look pale, Galina.

GALINA: Not used to such festivities. (*She obeys his gesture and sits next to him.*)

BERBENCHUK: All right, Glafira, my love . . . I'll do my best . . .

GLAFIRA: Anybody else, but not her!

GRIDNEV: Are you trying to get me drunk? The thing is, the more I drink, the soberer I get.

GLAFIRA: You can sniff around those two (*nodding at Katya and Olya*). I have a sixth sense, being a Soviet citizen. Do you know who she is? Have you examined her papers? (*She leads him to a group of people on the left.*)

MAIKOV: I was hoping to make friends with you. What a rotter you are.

GRIDNEV: Captain Maikov. It's late. Can you enlighten me? Are there guards at all the exits?

MAIKOV: At all the entrances.

GRIDNEV: No, I mean exits.

MAIKOV: This isn't a prison. It's a unit.

GRIDNEV: Is that so? (*Pointing to Galina.*) Just remember, if you let this girl escape, you'll get it in the neck.

MAIKOV (*rising, coldly*): Your papers?

GRIDNEV: Which?

MAIKOV: That little chit.

GRIDNEV: Er ... mm ... Counter-intelligence, you see, don't like to leave too many traces behind.

MAIKOV: In that case, I don't propose to be answerable for every passing girl.

GRIDNEV: You needn't be afraid. We never make a mistake. If someone is arrested, it's for a good reason.

MAIKOV: Never mind that. I'm an official, and I need a signature and a rubber stamp. (*He rises. Furiously*): You ... a-a-a-h ... You've ruined the party; spoiled all the fun. You've killed it; snuffed it out like a moth.

GRIDNEV: Since you're going, could you send the Commander to me.

MAIKOV: As far as I can see, you've only one stripe on your shoulder. (*He walks over to the window on the right.*)

GALINA (*to Vanin*): I met a lot of emigrés, I must confess. They were well-off, well fed, their houses comfortable. What were they missing? Why did they leave it all? What attracts them to our unkind, evil country? You enter a richly

furnished sitting room, and what do you see – a country
landscape with a ravine, a birch tree, a barn – and a wooden
fence. I once met an old landowner. Do you know what he
did when he arrived in Smolensk? He knelt down to kiss the
cobbles in front of the cathedral. This love of one's country!
It can't be understood, or cured, or justified. Some will be
hanged here; some will be imprisoned, but they keep flying
into the candle flame.

GRIDNEV (*beckons the Party Organiser*): An *operational* request,
Party Organiser. Send me the Divisional Commander, at
once.

The Party Organiser goes off to do so.

GALINA: As to the young people, they've taken their univer-
sity degrees there; they speak several European languages,
but marry their own kind. And they don't think for a minute
that they'll go on living abroad. For them – it's all for the time
being, for the time being . . .

Maikov summons Vanin to come over to the right.

OLYA (*taking part in a game, which has started up on the left of the
stage*): Forfeit! You must pay a forfeit for that.

BERBENCHUK (*approaching and bending over Gridnev*): You
wanted me, Comrade Lieutenant?

GRIDNEV: I did. Well, how are things? The state of
affairs . . .?

BERBENCHUK: Not too bad, on the whole . . .

GRIDNEV: How's the Division?

BERBENCHUK: On full alert, as you can see.

GRIDNEV: And how's Galina?

BERBENCHUK: Miss Pavlova? She's got what it takes, don't
you think?

GRIDNEV: She's a spy.

BERBENCHUK (*flabbergasted*): She's what?!

GRIDNEV: So you never spotted it?

*Galina shrinks from the glances on all sides. She turns nervously
first to Gridnev and Berbenchuk, then to Vanin and Maikov.*

GRIDNEV: You think you're good-natured. But to my mind

[72]

you're simply short-sighted. The girl just flicks her skirt, and you . . .

BERBENCHUK: Out of sheer boredom, don't you know. But I . . . Oh, dear . . .

GRIDNEV: You're spineless, that's what. Wherever you are, in the U.S.S.R., or abroad, you must perceive the enemy under any guise. Whoever you meet, man or woman, you must always think this might be an enemy. You must always be on the *qui vive*.

Maikov goes quickly out into the corridor. Vanin returns thoughtfully to Galina. A kind of line has been formed through Gridnev which separates Galina and Vanin from the rest of the company. The Head of the Chemical Unit who has been sitting throughout on the bottom step, with his face in his hands, lifts his head and recites:

HEAD OF THE CHEMICAL UNIT:

> Are you a prophet, or just a deceiver,
> Who constantly speaks of a new paradise?
> Stop your music, you mad organ grinder!
> I want to forget your song! Otherwise . . .

He lowers his head once again. Berbenchuk, utterly beside himself, moves away from Gridnev.

VANIN (*to Galina*): I'm very much afraid that these miles you have to cover on your way home will not be easy for you. You won't be received in a brotherly fashion: there'll be bayonets at the frontier. Let me give you a bit of advice. Get rid of all this jewelry and finery. When speaking of home, say 'ome. Use your fingers to blow your nose. Attach yourself to a party of peasant women, who are being herded home, frightened at being pushed around. Tie a scarf round your head, and put on an old country coat. Don't have a suitcase; carry a bag. Don't be squeamish about suet. Have some sausages with you, and some tobacco. There's no better friend than that, even if it doesn't last long. Whether it's the frontier guards, or the railway patrols, who don't want to let you in to the *Sovietische Union*, "Have a smoke" you say and generously fill their palms with it. They'd roll their cigarettes and ask: "Where are you from, girl?" "From Orlov," you'd say. They would chuck you under the chin and say "Off you go, you cow, we don't need your pass." You must forget everything you've seen – the forms of government, the customs, the differences, new ideas, dresses, even light and air – and when you get there, change your address; and if they ask if you've been under the occupation – the answer is, No.

Berbenchuk, as if afraid to cross the invisible line, stays downstage, and in a hoarse, theatrical whisper, tries to attract Vanin's attention.

BERBENCHUK: Major! Hey, Major!

VANIN: Eh?

BERBENCHUK: Vanin!

VANIN: What?

BERBENCHUK: Major!

VANIN: Well, what is it?

Berbenchuk is making signs.

VANIN: You come over here.

Berbenchuk refuses, desperately.

VANIN: Can't you? Oh, misery! I can hardly move my legs I've drunk so much.

Rising heavily, Vanin crosses the invisible line and leaves Galina finally alone. People on the left have imperceptibly disappeared – Anechka, Glafira, the Party Organiser, Prokopovich are gone. Galina has shrunk into herself. Gridnev keeps his eyes on her the whole time. The electric light grows dim, Vanin and Berbenchuk are downstage.

VANIN: What is it?

BERBENCHUK: Oh, my God, she's a spy.

VANIN: Who is?

BERBENCHUK: Shush, not so loud! We're lost!

VANIN: But, who?

BERBENCHUK: We! You. And I. After all you're my dep . . .

VANIN: Who's dep.? What's dep.? They'll start with you:

[74]

you're the chief. (*Berbenchuk is shattered. Vanin in a business-like manner*): Did the plenipotentiary say so?

BERBENCHUK: Yes.

VANIN: Has he got a warrant for her arrest?

BERBENCHUK: Seeing that he talks like that, maybe he has.

VANIN: You think he has. But coming here, he knew nothing about her.

BERBENCHUK: That's true. You're right.

VANIN: Go to bed. I'll wake you tomorrow.

BERBENCHUK (*in a weak voice*): Captain Maïkov.

VANIN: I'll tell him. You go to bed. Take your wife with you.

BERBENCHUK: With my darling Glafira! (*Is about to leave, but immediately turns back again.*)

VANIN: If you're not going, you'll have to deal with it yourself.

BERBENCHUK: Suppose I go to sleep, what sort of dreams shall I have? Still, I have some hope . . . You're good chaps, you two. (*Departing.*) The Division, it's lost! (*He meets Katya at the back of the stage and returns, holding her by an outstretched arm*): You'll sort it out, Arseniy?

VANIN: Of course I will.

BERBENCHUK: You've got me out of trouble. You're a good friend. But should anything . . . you know, don't knock on Glafira's door . . . She'll start looking for me . . . I'll be, so to speak, I'll be with Katya.

He departs with Katya. Likharyov and Olya are also gone. The light is ever growing dimmer.

GALINA (*fingering the phial round her neck*): I can hardly breathe. God, I'm terrified! Sergei is gone. All the friends have gone.

She steps back. Gridnev rises and advances upon her slowly. Vanin remains motionless downstage, in the centre. Suddenly, at the very top of the stairs there are loud footsteps, and almost immediately afterwards there is a pistol shot and the sound of broken glass. There is running about on the staircase – Maïkov, his head bandaged with a bloodstained cloth, waves an unsheathed sword, the Party Organiser behind him in his underclothes, getting dressed as he runs, and Saliy is holding a pistol above his head. They rush around the stage, infecting both Vanin and Gridnev with their panicky movements. Vanin minces around in a ludicrous manner. Some look through the windows.

MAIKOV (*shouting in snatches as he runs around the stage*): They've got through! The machine guns! I'm wounded. We're surrounded. There's only one escape route that isn't cut off!

In a kind of chain, all five, Vanin and Gridnev included, run off to the left. Saliy, being the last to go, shoots into the air once more. Galina rushes around, anxious, but relieved, and runs upstairs. The Head of the Chemical Unit lifts his head and looks around in amazement. The light is dim. Nerzhin enters from the right. He wears his great coat and a fur hat. His slow gait is out of tune with the pandemonium which has just taken place on the stage.

NERZHIN: They've gone, I see. (*Approaching the piano, he absent-mindedly plays a few notes.*)

THE HEAD OF THE CHEMICAL UNIT: Who was shooting here?

NERZHIN: You must have imagined it, you soak. (*The same depressing chords.*) Oh, chemist, chemist, where's your anti-gas? (*The same chord*). A typically Russian celebration. It started sideways and ended sadly.

THE HEAD OF THE CHEMICAL UNIT: Well, tell me something funny.

NERZHIN: Such as? . . . It was only today that I stood among the ruins (*we can hear music, which emanates from some unknown source*) of German glory . . . I think it was by chance that our army avoided going across the field which had a wooden sign, saying "Mines". I found not too far from Hohenstein newly blackened ruins, already sprinkled with snow.

Nerzhin is so taken up with his story that he fails to notice the departure of the Chemist, or Saliy's arrival and stealthy movements. He puts something under the corners of the carpet. Towards

[76]

*the end of his speech the light is so dim that the arc lights themselves
become visible.*

A memorial had been put up at the very edge, the very point
the Russian Army had reached and was surrounded thirty
years ago. Seven gloomy towers, to denote the number of
Wilhelm's divisions, linked by a wall with images of soldiers
set into it like saints, arrogant and still . . . Flag poles for
raising standards; a ceremonial arena; an altar at which
gloomy Teutonic oaths and speeches were made. The mob
used to come here to see their rulers. And suddenly it's all
blown up, the cold granite and uncaring marble are black-
ened by the smoke of the explosion. There is a yawning gap
in the ring of wall, some towers flattened, others still stand-
ing like skeletons . . . Having had one victorious moment,
they thought, in their madness, they would last forever.
There I stood, by Hindenburg's vault, an enemy soldier,
neither proud nor happy, with a tired smile on my lips,
thinking how absurd human vanity is, how disgusting . . .in
the midst of the countryside. The branches of trees,
momentarily shaken by the blast, are again covered with
star-like flakes of snow. You may have been a glorious
Commander, you may have received all the honours, but
what are your diamond, star-studded and brilliant medals
compared to this silent and reconciling snow.

*Lieutenant Yachmennikov appears in the right hand door. He
wears his great coat, with a leather belt and a fur hat. He is slender
and young; all white from the snow. At first he stands in the
doorway, then enters quietly.*

A tangle of eternal injuries! You triumph, then you weep,
then triumph again. If only we could learn the lesson of this
generous earth of how to *forget* . . . Oh, you inglorious
enemy of my people, how can I get through to you against
that wall of incomprehension? Look, Germany, what your
evil triumphs have led to. Today it is we who rejoice, like
Balthasar. But what retribution, what wrath are we sowing
for our children? Oh, innocent Russia, demented

Russia . . . Yachmennikov! Ooo, you're all covered with snow!

YACHMENNIKOV (*officially*): Comrade Captain, the engines are still running. The whole battery has arrived. What are your orders?

NERZHIN: Sit down. Where are the men?

YACHMENNIKOV: I've brought them into the house.

NERZHIN: Soon we'll be off: to fight.

YACHMENNIKOV: What's all this? On that mirror?

NERZHIN: Ever read the Bible?

YACHMENNIKOV: My mother used to. And father read it on Holy Days. As for us, we spent our time studying the Shorter Manual.

NERZHIN: Should you live, do read it. Today it's the Major's birthday.

YACHMENNIKOV: Is that so? Well, he's a good man. One could wish such a . . .

NERZHIN: Let's drink to him.

YACHMENNIKOV: Shouldn't I switch the engines off?

NERZHIN: Let them tick over quietly: we're not that poor. Apart from the Baku oilwells, we possess Ploesti[19] now. What will you drink? There's some nice Corsican wine here, such as we've never tasted, you and I.

Yachmennikov looks at himself in the mirror.

What are you looking at?

YACHMENNIKOV: I'm just checking if they'll know me at home.

NERZHIN: Your parents will. But I doubt if the girl friends will. As I remember you from your student days, you've become a man. And what, Victor, are you going to tell them at your village council in Godunov, and your friends of the Vladimir district? Will you tell them how we followed in Rokossovsky's footsteps; how we ate our dinner off a mirror – will they ever believe it?

YACHMENNIKOV: It wouldn't do to talk about such things in our village.

NERZHIN: So what shall we drink to, you conqueror? If you live, you'll get home, and get married, and propagate the tribe – who doesn't do that? Let's think of something special, something original. What is your special wish?

YACHMENNIKOV: Special, special? ... That somehow or other they would disband the collective farms.

NERZHIN: Abandon the collective farms! I must say! You're no fool. But since that's the toast you want, raise your glass. *They drink.*
But, you know, Marx did write that it would be best not to disturb the successful peasants. For them Communism is unknown territory, a sort of Mars. Disband the collective farms! It's all talk, Victor, it's palliatives. They babble on to persuade you to face those iron tanks.

YACHMENNIKOV: I look at it that way, too. Those collective farms are useful to the State, not to us. Without them the State wouldn't get a grain out of us peasants. They wouldn't be able to do a thing.

NERZHIN: Well, you old castle. Did you hear our toast? Up with the Russians! I'll pour you some of this vintage wine: the bottle is all dusty ... And I'll tell you what *my* dreams are: that in Russia you could say out loud whatever you think. That's not going to happen soon, eh?

YACHMENNIKOV: Not too soon, I expect.

NERZHIN: What if it does?
They clink their glasses and drink.
Now you drink to any Major you like. I've had enough, even before these two glasses. But help yourself. Fill your pockets!
(Shoving food towards him. Yachmennikov declines.)

YACHMENNIKOV: Comrade Captain, our cars are chock-a-block!

NERZHIN: Oh, hell, I forgot. I come from a starving district. Will we ever get rid of this greed? Well, brother, let's roll on further across Europe. Don't put my Blitz-Opel in front. I'm taking a girl with me. Don't ... don't look at me like that.

YACHMENNIKOV: How do you mean, like that? I'm not looking like that.

NERZHIN: But thinking?

YACHMENNIKOV: I'm thinking that there're three front seats . . .

NERZHIN: I bet you're thinking the Battery Commander is at it at last. But no, old friend, she's engaged to someone else. *Yachmennikov stands to attention, salutes and turning in a military manner, leaves. Nerzhin moves slowly towards the staircase, but on hearing a noise from above, runs upstairs. There enter quickly, and in a preoccupied manner, Vanin with grenades and a cartridge belt; Gridnev carrying an automatic weapon (he doesn't know how to carry it or sling it and is in constant danger of either killing himself or his companions); the Party Organiser who carries a rifle with a bayonet. Behind him, Maikov in ceremonial uniform, still with a bandage round his head as before. He's pulling a heavy machine gun by a rope with one hand, while in the other he carries a sword. This whole scene is uneasy, under moving searchlights.*

VANIN (*smoking a pipe*): No panic. Stay calm. We are unbeatable. Captain Maikov, you must maintain radio contact with us.

MAIKOV: Everybody down!

He, Gridnev and the Party Organiser throw themselves down. Vanin imperturbably continues to stand, smoking. A sizzling fire-cracker explodes upwards from underneath the carpet.

VANIN: Well, well, the infernal machine hasn't exploded yet.

All three rise. Thereafter, Gridnev and the Party Organiser move with great caution. Maikov, having unsheathed his sword, waves it around.

MAIKOV: Boy, what a sword! Party Organiser, shall we chop them down Cossack fashion? Want to take it? (*He ties the sword to the Party Organiser's belt.*) Vlad, you dare-devil! Take the machine gun at least! (*He shoves the rope of the machine gun into Gridnev's hand.*)

GRIDNEV (*pushing it away*): What am I to do with it? I've . . . no idea.

MAIKOV: Then let me give you a Maxim gun and three hundred bullets.

VANIN: Calm yourself, Lieutenant. Remember what Chapayev[20] used to say. What should a Communist do at a moment like this?

THE PARTY ORGANISER: Enough of this demagogy! We are the leaders. Our lives are precious to the people.

VANIN: That's just what I'm saying. Into the car, I say! Be off with you!

They move towards the exit. Maikov, stretching out his arms, stops them leaving.

MAIKOV: You'll get lost! To be on the safe side, take a map at least.

GRIDNEV (*pushing it away*): I don't know how to read a map.

MAIKOV: So what did they teach you?

GRIDNEV: The principles of Leninism. Spy-ology. The history of the Party . . .

With an awkward movement, he steps on another fire-cracker: it sizzles and goes off.

MAIKOV: Oh, dear, how careless. But I'm glad you've survived your baptism by fire!

VANIN: Party Organiser! Don't panic! Who shall stay here to maintain the Party rule?

MAIKOV: When you return, you'll have to bury our corpses.

VANIN: No panic. I open the conference of the Party Group. (*He climbs on a chair, puts one foot on the mirror, and leans on one knee.*) *Gridnev and the Party Organiser approach Vanin. Maikov moves away.* Comrades! Just one question: which of the three of us shall stay behind in the Division, as Party link? I suggest Gridnev.

Everybody looks at Gridnev.

GRIDNEV (*animatedly*): Comrade Deputy Commander. Considering . . . (*He searches his pockets.*) Here's my medical certificate . . . My health is poor . . .

VANIN: Who, then?

GRIDNEV: Party Organiser, you wouldn't mind . . .

THE PARTY ORGANISER: Hey, no! I can't either. I would suggest Likharyov.

VANIN: But where is he?

MAIKOV: With a girl, somewhere.

THE PARTY ORGANISER: In that . . . case – the Staff Captain.

GRIDNEV (*shifting his automatic awkwardly*): Stop squabbling, for goodness sake. We shall all be taken prisoner.

MAIKOV (*rushes towards him and moves the barrel down*): For God's sake, keep it down!

VANIN (*in the same position, completely cool*). He (*nods at Maikov*) can't be left. He's not a *member*. He's only a candidate.
Maikov guiltily lowers his head.
Or shall we trust him? Maikov!
Maikov raises his head. He grows in stature noticeably with each phrase.

THE PARTY ORGANISER: The Party!

GRIDNEV: Over to you!

VANIN: Completely!

THE PARTY ORGANISER: Great trust!

GRIDNEV: A big responsibility!

VANIN: You'll lead the fighters . . .

THE PARTY ORGANISER: In the sacred cause of Comrade Stalin!

GRIDNEV: You'll be in charge of the Commander's Units.

THE PARTY ORGANISER: And you must see to it that the organisation should grow. New recruits!

VANIN (*getting off his pedestal*): Where the hell's my pipe? I'm too old to go off travelling in the middle of the night . . .

SALIY AND ZAMALIY (*come running in together*): The car is ready!
Gridnev and the Party Organiser both start rushing. Vanin pushes them along.

VANIN: Go, go! For Stalin! For Mother Russia!

*They go out left. Zamaliy, at a sign from Maikov, noisily pushes
out the machine gun in the same direction. Maikov is alone. His
cheerful excitement evaporates. He stands pensively, then pulls off
his bandage, moves over to the piano, leans despondently on it.
Nerzhin appears at the top of the staircase with an elegant ladies'
suitcase in his hand. Maikov sees him.*

MAIKOV: Et tu Brute! Looting! It's a nightmare . . .

NERZHIN: I'm off, Alex.

MAIKOV: Be off, then.

NERZHIN: So long!

MAIKOV: Au revoir!

*Nerzhin stands more than halfway up the staircase. Galina, in a
fur coat, joins him silently. Maikov can now see her as well. He
whistles, then leaning on the music stand, with his back to it, he
smiles and sings:*

> Having climbed his rickety bridge,
>
> He remembers the port he has left . . .

*Nerzhin and Galina, arm in arm, descend the stairs, the spotlights
following them:*

ALL THREE: And flicks off the foam of the sea

> From his naval and elegant boots!

Exeunt right, waving to Maikov, who waves back.

CURTAIN

1951
Ekibastuz
Composed orally while on gang labour.

TRANSLATORS' NOTES

1. Vassily Surikov, 19th-century painter.

2. Theodossiya Morozova, member of the Old Believers Sect: starved to death for her beliefs in 1672. Subject of Surikov's dramatic picture.

3. A line from a poem by Alexander Blok (1880–1921).

4. Alexander Suvorov, famous Russian General (1729–1800).

5. Zoya Kosmodemyanskaya (1923–41), Heroine of the USSR, executed by the Germans.

6. V. V. Mayakovsky (1894–1930), Futurist poet.

7. Russian Liberation Army, set up under the aegis of the Wehrmacht, headed by General A. Vlasov and consisting of the Soviet prisoners of war and White émigrés, in the hope of liberating Russia from Bolshevik rule.

8. Gori, a town in Georgia, north-west of Tbilisi, Stalin's birthplace.

9. Magnitogorsk, a town in the Urals.

10. Potyomkin, a reference to fictional villages created by Prince Potyomkin (1739–91) to impress Catherine the Great.

11. K. K. Rokossovsky (1896–1968), Marshal. Twice Hero of the USSR. Deputy Minister of Defence and Chief Inspector of the Armed Forces.

12. General A. V. Samsonov (1859–1914), Commander of the Second Army on the Eastern Front in the First World War.

13. N. I. Bukharin (1888–1938), leading Bolshevik, purged and executed.

14. K. F. Gauss (1777–1855), German mathematician.

15. N. I. Yezhov (1895–1938), Commissar of Internal Affairs.

16. M. V. Lomonosov (1711–65), a peasant's son, Professor of Chemistry and Physics, member of the Academy of Sciences.

17. A. A. Vlasov, General in the Red Army, taken prisoner in 1942. Head of the Russian Liberation Army. Arrested by the Soviets in 1945, executed the following year.

18. A. Vertinsky, émigré 'diseur', returned to the USSR after the War.

19. Ploesti, Roumanian oil-field.

20. V. I. Chapayev (1887–1919), Bolshevik Hero of the Civil War.